She openeth her
mouth with wisdom;
and in her tongue is the
law of kindness. Her
children arise up, and call
her blessed;
Proverbs 1:26,28a KJV

Presented to:

_____

From:

_____

Date:

_____

Treasures From a Mother's Heart

A Celebration of Memories from
One Generation to Another

Written By
Donna Kauffman

Eerdman's Printing Company
Grand Rapids, Michigan

For more information:
Donna Kauffman
19151 Hobart Road
West Farmington, Ohio 44491
kauffman@modex.com
1-440-548-5436

The following articles (with rights now having returned to the author) were first published in the following magazine/websites:

Where Are We (First published in Christian Families Online, feature 58) © by Donna Kauffman

Grand Slam Snowball Fight (First published in Mennonite Brethren Herald Vol. 40, No. 11) © by Donna Kauffman

Tea Parties (First published in Christian Mirror.com/recipes, 7/26/2001) © by Donna Kauffman

An Amazing Mother (First published in History's Women.com/Admire29, 7/25/2001) © by Donna Kauffman

Backyard Camping (First published in Joyfull Noise, June/July 2002) © by Donna Kauffman

ISBN: 0-9722411-0-8

Printed in the U. S. A. by
Eerdman's Printing Company
Grand Rapids, Michigan 49601

This book is dedicated to my daughters
and grandchildren with love from
their mother's heart:
Carla, Rachel, and Christa,
my little girls grown big,
and to my tiny grandchildren:
Kyle, Sierra and Kassondra.

May you experience the message the Lord
has woven in each story of your lives.

Acknowledgments

I owe gratitude to my faithful supporters:

My husband Bob. He has been my encourager, prayer partner, best friend, believer of my dreams, listener and wise counselor.

My daughters, Carla, Rachel and Christa. Carla took my efforts for a title and created the perfect one. The girls carefully studied each story more times than we care to count and kept me encouraged with their prayers and kind words.

My sons-in-law, Rod Schwartz and Glen Zehr. Each allowed me to read story after story to them with pleasant expressions that cheered me on.

My mother, Iris Zook. Mom believed in my writing, read many of my stories and often talked of a book.

My sister, Norma Grieser. Her enthusiasm and continual promptings to compile my stories into a book — well before I even considered the concept kept me dreaming.

My niece, Shari Ladd. Shari carefully and insightfully did my layout, final editing and cover design for almost nothing in return. I'm afraid I'll be indebted to her forever! (Newsletter editor for Michigan State University)

My friend, Sharon Kuepfer. She wouldn't let my dream die and diligently edited my work. (Author of Home Schooling Moments and Child-Friendly Recipes)

My proofreaders, Carol Ramer, Joyce Grieser, Norma Grieser and April Swartz. They spent hours studying the manuscript, correcting errors and encouraging me forward.

My photographer, Joann Kauffman. Joann listened to my thoughts and came up with the creative cover idea and took the excellent snapshot. Other photos by Joann are on pages 3 and 100.

Table of Contents

Treasured Memories

January 3, 2001 numbered three days of continual pain in my lower abdomen. I wasn't feeling well enough to work that day so I sat down and began jotting goals for the New Year. I didn't get beyond the one aim of "looking to find a treasure hidden in every day throughout the year."

I made the decision late that afternoon to go to the emergency room to have my persistent ache checked out. Test results showed gall stones had seeped out into unhealthy places, resulting in a severe case of pancretitis. During the next nine days, I floated in and out of a drugged semi-conscious state. Concerns involved whether the pancreas would either begin to heal itself or take my life. I sensed the uncertainty of my physical condition, and in my deep, dark, medicated mind the idea of "treasures" continually surfaced – always with a specific blessing attached.

I felt a struggle between my fleshly desire to continue on this earth and what the ultimate plan of God might be. Unable to coherently think for extended periods of time, there were a few brief seconds when I was able to consciously choose to commit myself to whatever the Lord had for me. His presence was so real as He continued to bless me with yet another treasured gift that I was able to know in my heart that I wanted whatever He knew was best for me.

As I began my recovery process, the reality of what all had taken place set in. I came home very weak, extremely thankful and with the resolve that I would get my treasures on paper. I began writing memories from the nine intense days of struggle in the hospital back to when my daughters were tiny up to today with my three beloved grandchildren. A year and a half later, this book is born.

Woven in the fabric of everyday living, the Lord paints a message. A message of strength, promise and hope. Each jaunt of my pilgrimage has been filled with delightful joy and, at times, regrets. I invite you to come along with me on this journey of treasured memories and note the nugget of truth hidden in each reflection. I hope you will open the diary of your own heart and feel the sense of the Lord's promise and His love in the remembrance of each of your experiences.

Section One

Tiny Daughters

Lo, children are an heritage of the Lord.
~ Psalm 127:3 KJV ~

Sunday Afternoon Strolls

Each day comes bearing its own gifts. Untie the Ribbons.
~ Ruth Ann Shabacker ~

Sunday afternoon strolls were a favorite when our daughters were young. We found it a great way to enjoy the glory of God's creation on a quiet Sunday.

Cold winter walks meant extra time for the bundling of warm cloaks. The clear sky above and the crisp snow crunching under foot made the extra work well worth it. Early spring Sunday jaunts were priceless; the warmth after those very long cold months can not be forgotten. The fair weather days, likely not above 40 degrees, called not only for the three girls to go on a stroll, but for dollies in their carriages as well. Baby dolls were dressed in just the right outerwear and wrapped snuggly in cozy blankets. They were placed tenderly in their strollers and out the door the three buggies went, each followed by a young lady.

These little outings were small things; however, they were memory builders and tiny threads that weave together the person we become tomorrow. Though to me, 40 degrees felt too cold for walks, it was priceless to watch little girls bundle their babies and haul them along for these chilly spring hikes.

By wisdom a house is built, and through understanding it's established;
through knowledge its rooms are filled with rare and beautiful treasures.
~ Proverbs 24:3-4 ~

Homemaking on the Deck

Parenthood is a partnership with God. You are not molding iron nor chiseling marble; you are working with the Creator of the universe in shaping human character and determining destiny.

~ Ruth Vaughn ~

Our back deck was transformed into three small homes one early spring day. The long, cold winter months in northern Ontario made the first sunshiny day above 45 degrees a day for being outdoors.

Bright and early in the day, my three daughters felt the vast wide earth calling them. Donned with warm sweaters, sweatshirts and furry hats, the trio began their process. From the bedroom, into the dining room, on through the living room, out the back door and onto the deck went the parade. Their arms were laden with every sort of item needed for homemaking.

The deck was just the right size for their three houses. Two-year-old Christa sat her doll bed in the first corner. One baby lay sleeping while another was propped in the infant seat on a chair. Diapers and clothes were changed as needed. The next spot found 6-year-old Rachel making a chair out of a cardboard box and pillows. Her dollies had their beds close by and rested nicely between feedings. The bottles and clothes were neatly stashed in an imaginary cupboard. Seven-year-old Carla busily fixed, arranged and organized the tiny table and chairs with matching dishes in the center. Her babies were content to play quietly as she did the week's worth of ironing for her brood.

Two of the sisters planned a trip to visit the other, who lived far away. The necessary phone calls were made and the weekend visit was set. The bulging diaper bags held every essential item needed for a road trip and the pretend moms and children were off. Through the opened living room door I could hear stories of reminiscing and gales of laughter as the three caught up on one another's lives.

At the close of this make believe mothering day, the playing house was over and so was the fun. Moving inside and stashing each item back into place took some probing, encouragement and help on mom's part. As I tucked my daughters into bed that night, I whispered a prayer that when my little girls were grown up, they would know this kind of sibling joy and mothering delight with their very own real doll babies. That would make all the work, mess and fuss of today well worth it. ⟩⟨

To be ... keepers at home,
~ Titus 2:5 KJV ~

Tea Parties

*Somehow, taking tea together encourages an atmosphere of intimacy
when you slip off the time piece in your mind and cast your fate
to a delight of tasty tea, tiny foods, and thoughtful conversation.*
~ Gail Greco ~

Growing up over the years, my three young daughters loved tea parties. At age 2 and 3, Carla and best friend Mary were often found setting the table with an itsy, bitsy teapot and some make believe snacks. Together the team would chatter, giggle and sip empty teacups  while munching pretend cookies. Frequently, younger sister Rachel would wish for tea with real tea biscuits, so the tiny table for her party was carefully set. She and her little sister Christa would relish in the actual thing. Many times in those early years, I'd watch these cherubs set their table full of doll babies with a chair left for each of them. The make believe people made tea most pleasant for these wee girls.

One grand day 3-year-old Christa invited two of her favorite adult friends to tea. Dragging her small table to the middle of the kitchen, along with chairs and the miniature tea set, she was ready for her guests to arrive. At exactly 2:00 pm, Ruby and Erma stepped into the aroma-filled kitchen and gathered together with Christa on the tiny chairs. This trio sipped genuine tea from the tiny china cups. The chit chat and laughter was most contagious as I stood by observing from the kitchen counter.

15

There were times when the girls' daddy was doing some work around home and the trio prepared a little tea time for him. On many occasions, when my daughters would return from school, I'd have the table set and ready with china cups and fresh baked rolls. These were happy times of sharing all about our day with each other.

Today, with each Bible Study group or individual friend that enters my home, teacups come out along with a simple treat. We adults enter into the pleasantries that a delicate tea party offers. Hopefully tea time for my children and friends will always be a time when each can revert to the happy go lucky childhood days and once more unburden their hearts. 🍵

A friend loves at all times.
~ Proverbs 17:17a ~

Angels Shall Keep Her

As a mother, I must faithfully, patiently, lovingly and
happily do my part - then wait quietly for God to do His.
~ Ruth Bell Graham ~
(Prodicals and Those Who Love Them)

Christa, who was a year and a half, generally wore a large bubbling smile. She loved life and lived it with vigor.

One day I looked out the window and saw Christa playing with her sister Carla. Behold, there she was, standing so very high with one foot on each of the handlebars of the glider swing. Her smile was bigger than ever as she swung herself as hard and fast as she could.

This marked the nature of my little girl—friendly, daring and full of fun. I can't begin to number how many times I've bowed in thankful prayer that—

He shall give His angels charge over thee [her],
and keep thee [her] in all Thy ways.
~ Psalm 91:11 KJV ~

Dear Lord, thank you that I can trust my children with your powerful love and protection. Amen

The Tipped Over Plant

Sometimes we as mothers learn life's lessons from our little girls. Often it is in their childlike faith that the greatest lessons are learned.

~ Ginny Hobson ~

Rachel, just 12 months old, wandered up to me in the kitchen one day. Unable to talk yet, my daughter solemnly showed me her dirty hands and motioned for me to follow her. As I walked behind the tottering little girl, she kept glancing back to be sure I was following. We paraded through the dining room, into the living room and way over by the window until Rachel stopped next to a tipped over plant. She gravely pointed to the results of her misdeed and again showed me her messy hands.

Rachel knew the plants were off limits. I marveled at how such a tiny one could sense her guilt and bring her confession to her mother, well before she was using words. Cleaning up the unpleasant mess relieved Rachel, and feeling forgiven, free of her burden and clean, she cheerfully toddled off to play.

This all spoke to me about learning to go to the Lord quickly to confess a wrong. I tend to carry the burden of my guilt for to long, yet Rachel came to me right away to correct her wrong. I want to learn from this tiny one to go immediately to the Master when I've failed. The look of relief on Rachel's face when the consequence of her misdeed was all cleaned up will serve as a reminder to me forever; there is freedom in forgiveness. 🍃

Though your sins are as scarlet, they shall be as white as snow.
~ Isaiah 1:18 ~

Just Like Daddy

Example is not the main thing in influencing others.
It's the only thing.
~ Albert Schweitzer ~

One quiet evening Bob laid stretched out on the living room floor reading a newspaper. Minutes later, he beckoned me to take a peek. There beside him, in as much the same manner as her daddy, lay little 2-year-old Carla. She was on her tummy—just like daddy, propped up on elbows—just like daddy, magazine held right before her face—just like daddy.

At such a tiny age, Carla sought to be just like her daddy, copying his every move. How challenged Bob and I felt to plant the values of the Word deep in our hearts and live as much like Jesus as Carla wanted to live - just like her daddy.

Train a child in the way he should go,
and when he is old he will not turn from it.
~ Proverbs 22:6 ~

A Perfect Fall Afternoon

*Blessed and praised be the Lord, from whom comes all
the good that we speak and think and do.*
~ *Teresa of Avila* ~
(The Way of Protection)

It was a perfectly quiet fall afternoon. Not a ripple could be seen in the beautiful blue lake that spread beyond our back yard. The only sound came from the occasional loon flapping across it, calling out his special cry. I glanced out the window, sensing the same stillness in my heart that could always be felt when observing the wonder of God's vast creation in our northern Ontario home. There, at the edge of the yard, Rachel and her favorite friend Hans sat in a wheelbarrow surrounded by a bouquet of golden sunflowers. One by one, the two were pulling individual seeds from these perfectly formed, bright yellow, fall treats.

I was awed with the splendor of God's handiwork in nature, mingled with the glory and innocence of a child created in the very image of our loving God. ✺

Be still, and know that I am God.
~ Psalm 46:10 ~

Delightful Dandelions

God is in the details.

~ Ludwig Mies ~

The warmth of early summer days mixed with a bright sunny field of golden dandelions gives a sense of quiet stillness in my heart. On one such day as this my two young daughters went out to play. Carla, a lively 2 year old, and Rachel, not quite 1, sat together in a delightful patch of those undesirable dandelions. Something about the charm of my two little girls sitting among those weeds has changed my perception of the brilliantly colored, but troublesome plants.

So great is the wonder that even deep, dark, distressing days in my life can likewise become glorious. Oswald Chambers writes, "The meaning of prayer is that we get hold of God, not of the answer." I find as I move to the Lord in a troublesome weedy time, I meet God in a way that I'm okay without an answer to my plea. His presence feels as blissful to me as my little girls looked in that patch of annoying dandelions.

If you return to the Almighty you will be restored.
~ Job 22:23 ~

Praises to the Lord

*Angels listen for your songs, for your voice rises to the very
gates of heaven when you praise Me.*
~ Frances J. Roberts ~

Many years ago, when our daughters were young, there was a
host of small children in our church. Each Sunday morning these
cherubs would stand at the front of the chapel and sing praise songs to
the Lord.

Oh how they loved this one:
Keep me Jesus as the apple of thine eye,
Hide me under the shadow of thy wings;
Keep thy hand upon me lest I die,
Keep me Jesus as the apple of thine eye.

Another all time favorite, sung with arms lifted in motion, to the
message was:
From the rising of the sun,
To the going down of the same,
The Name of the Lord is to be praised;
Praise ye the Lord.

At the front of this rustic chapel was a door that led to the
outside. At times the children would lean back against it as they sang.
One particular morning Christa was leaning against the door. It so
happened that morning that the door was not latched properly and to
everyone's amazement, 4-year-old Christa tumbled backwards out the
opening. She was a little embarrassed, but not hurt. Christa's fun-loving
personality naturally brought encouragement from everyone. She was
helped back to her spot and the praise songs continued. Without further
teaching, the children learned to stand up straight and away from the
door for Sunday morning praises. 🎵

From the lips of children and infants you have ordained praise.
~ Matthew 21:16 ~

Sunday is a Holy Day

May God help us to train our children in godly principles!
~ Elizabeth Elliot ~

Every Sunday morning we were up early preparing for church. Breakfast was eaten and faces were washed. Hair was neatly combed and fresh colorful dresses buttoned on little girls. Carla, 3, and Rachel, 2, often clothed as twins, toted their little purse with pen and paper in one hand and each carried their tiny Bible in their other hand.

We held Sunday sacred in our home according to the third commandment. We didn't spend it sitting on straight back chairs quietly meditating as those of long ago did, but we did set it aside as a day for worship, learning from the scriptures, resting and doing quiet family things.

In a world that is fast losing its grip on Biblical values, I pray that our reverence on the day established for rest would carry on through the next generation and the next. 🙰

To [those] who keep my Sabbaths, who choose what please me and hold fast to my covenant— these I will bring to my holy mountain and give them joy in my house of prayer.
~ Isaiah 56:4,7 ~

Jesus Loves Me

Anna B. Warner

Jesus loves me! This I know,
For the Bible tells me so;
Little ones to Him belong;
They are weak but He is strong.

(Chorus)
Yes, Jesus loves me;
Yes, Jesus loves me;
Yes, Jesus loves me;
The Bible tells me so.

Jesus loves me! He who died,
Heaven's gate to open wide;
He will wash away my sin,
Let His little child come in.

Jesus loves loves me! loves me still,
Tho' I'm very weak and ill;
From His shining throne on high,
Comes to watch me where I lie.

A Hungry Little Girl

Forgiveness is the first step on the road to a fresh start.

Tiny Rachel, not yet a year old, was hungry. This toddler found a loaf of bread nearly as large as she and slowly, but determinedly, she carried that package on her unsteady feet across several rooms to where I was working. Rachel wasn't yet talking so she passed the heavily spilling bag over with a look of "please mommy?" I took the loaf of bread and promptly got my daughter something to fill her need.

Rachel sensed her physical wish for food as she knew it would meet her desire. This little scenario reminded me of the desperation I had felt a few days before. I went to Psalm 103:11 and the Lord showed me that His love for me is as high as the heavens are above the earth. That promise quieted my aching heart just as food satisfied Rachel's physical pain. I remembered once again that He is my bread from heaven and He satisfies my every need.

Man does not live on bread alone, but on every word
that comes from the mouth of God.
~ Matthew 4:4 ~

Where Are We

Lie on your back in the freshly cut grass and count the stars in the midnight navy sky – and know there is much of life yet to discover and enjoy.

Our family was on a seminar trip with the purpose of teaching family life principles, singing and sharing at several Inuit communities. Everyone was wrapped in heavy parkas and hats, along with our extra warm mukluks, or boots, and our mittens, which were made of moose hide and lined with the warmest of fabric. We huddled together in the cold eight-seat plane and flew uneventfully for several hours.

We spent several days in polar bear country well beyond the tree line, close to the icy Arctic Circle. While at one small community, we observed the large hide of a freshly killed polar bear. We learned about "Eskimo" ice cream, which was different than we expected as it was made of whipped whale blubber.

One thoughtful couple served us an area delicacy of arctic char, a two-foot long fish that was freshly caught and placed promptly into a freezer. During our visit in their home it was carried to the table and big chunks of the frozen, raw meat were sliced off and passed to each person to enjoy.

Another encouraging part of our journey was sharing with the handful of believers there. As we visited and shared together it was intriguing to observe the babies in the large pouches of their mothers' ever-warm outerwear.

We made our final jaunt of some hours further north to visit with an elderly pastor couple who had made their home among the Inuit people for over 50 years. We were so far into the blustery cold barren arctic, that for miles, nothing could be seen but blue sky above and white frozen earth beneath.

Upon yet another safe, comfortable landing in the twin engine Seneca, we stumbled out of the plane. Christa, hardly five-years-old, bundled in her overweight wraps and with her toque down over her eyes, leaned against the nose of that big bird, peered up and out from under her hat and queried, "Daddy, where are we?" Her desperate plea brought chuckles as we began to explain to this young one exactly where we were while standing on this landing strip in the middle of what seemed like no where.

We had quite the hands-on geography lesson about this vast earth. Christa and her sisters realized there are people everywhere in this world and that the Lord lives in the hearts of people wherever we go. We felt very blessed to know that the Lord is with us in all places.

For the Lord your God will be with you wherever you go.
~ Joshua 1:9 ~

Busy Laundry Day

*Then do not grasp at the stars, but do life's plan, common work as it comes,
certain that daily duties and daily bread are the sweetest things in life.*
~ Robert Louise Stevenson ~

Busy laundry days for mommy meant the same for little girls.
All the doll clothes were gathered and heaped into the laundry basket.
The red sleeper was actually a baby gift from Great Aunt Fern when
4-year-old Carla was a baby. It now fit one of her life-sized dolls. There
were also home sewn garments in the basket that another aunt had
created. The aqua-colored sleeper was a baby gift for Rachel, who had
recently turned 3.

The collection of these
miniature articles was tucked
one by one into the washing
machine and the exact amount of
soap was carefully measured
and poured into the tub. The
one-half hour wait while the
washer ran its cycle found the
busy young ladies hauling the
large clothes rack out the door to
the back yard.

At last, the assortment of
clothing had spun out finishing
the washing process in the noisy
machine. With a chair pushed
tight up against it and little girls
propped on top, each article was dug from the washer. Together the
team tugged and lugged that heavy load out to the awaiting clothes rack.
The ambitious girls carefully shook out each wee garment and hung
them over the rods. The sunshine brightened and dried the day's worth
of work, while wearied girls rested from their labors.

Surely acting out these household tasks as tiny tots will prepare them in virtues for years to come. Oh, it's some extra work and mess on mom's part, but for future blessings I'll rest in the clutter as my little laundress's labor and sing:

Shaking mats and scrubbing floors,
In the house and out of doors,
Washing, ironing, mending too,
these are things that girls can do.
I'll do it all for Jesus,
I'll do it all for Jesus,
I'll do it all for Jesus,
He's done so much for me.

Let the favor of the Lord be upon us and prosper for us
the work of our hands.
~ Psalm 90:17 ~

Fun-Filled Little Girls

*Two persons must believe in each other, and feel that it can be done
and must be done; in that way they are enormously strong.
They must keep each other's courage.*

~ Vincent Van Gogh ~

Rachel invited her friend Heidi over to play one warm summer day. These little girls were full of spirit and energy. Their imaginations were certainly bigger than their age of five years.

After some time of outdoor play the gleeful pair meandered to the house. What a sight I saw. Big bright smiles beamed above blackened and muddied, once white arms and legs. Wet soil in northern Ontario is thick, gooey and dark gray. What fun it had been to paint their tiny white arms and legs with that black goop!

After posing for good-natured pictures we sprayed crystal clear water over the fun-filled team. Slowly little white hands reappeared and then thin white arms shone out. During this clean up process I caught a glimpse of the blackness of my selfish sins. I imagined the blood of the Lamb washing over me and making me whiter than these tiny arms and legs once again became. I joyfully burst out and sang this little song:

Though your sins be as scarlet,
they shall be as white as snow.
~ Isaiah 1:18 KJV ~

Family Night

~~~~~

Make a memory with your children;
Spend some time to show you care.
Toys and trinkets can't replace those
Precious moments that you share.
~ Elaine Hardt ~

Every Tuesday evening we celebrated the family and called it "family night." Weekly, our daughters would take turns to be in charge of this special evening.

The little one in charge had several big responsibilities to take care of. First, she needed to plan the dinner menu. What a variety of meals we had. Hot dogs with macaroni and cheese was a favorite and once we made the cutest little strawberry shortcake sandwiches. When the planned menu consisted of all desserts, mom stepped in with some assistance.

The evening activity came after dinner. These girls were creative as they took their turn making the plans. We played store with Rachel dressed up in her cashier's jacket and real food boxes lining make believe shelves. The noisily ringing cash register was kept very busy opening and closing as customer's purchased and repurchased carts full of groceries.

On some of these evenings we had Miss Nurse visit us. With her nurse cap and apron properly in place, Carla would gently give a shot to her daddy for his bronchitis. She would bandage her sisters severely broken arm, take our blood pressure and pass out candy pills to each patient in need.

Other evenings we piled into the family car and made the trip to the local library. Each of the girls selected their stack of books and their dad carefully reviewed each one. A stop at the new McDonalds for a 25-cent ice cream treat topped those evenings off splendidly. The rare occasion found us at the 7-eleven store where 50-cent slurpies were our treasure. We had one for each person, since there was no sharing special snacks on family night.

At the close of these delightful evenings, the daughter in charge led the family worship. Christa was excellent at getting everyone involved in acting out Bible stories. We sang action songs and now and then a hymn. We always ended with prayer time led in a variety of different ways.

We'll treasure these family night memories as long as our minds can remember. Bob was a better patient on the "nurse" evenings than I was. Actually, he acted out the baby role during playing house night splendidly. I found it more difficult to enjoy these playtimes as much as Bob did, but I'll never regret protecting Tuesday evenings for family night. Possibly these same little girls, grown up, will carry this tradition on to their own families.

Train up a child in the way he should go,
and when he is old he will not turn from it.
~ Proverbs 22:6 ~

Carla's Catch

Fly across the lonely years,
And old home scenes of my childhood,
In fond memory appears.
~ J.B.F. Wright ~

We donned our young family in bright orange life jackets, hopped aboard the small fishing boat and pushed from shore. Carla, 3, and Rachel, 2, were casting their fishing lines into the water and anxiously awaiting a bite. The natural beauty of the forest surrounding Crystal Lake along with the perfect blue sky, mirrored in the peaceful water, was breathtaking.

As we wondered at the beauty our hushed silence was abruptly broken when Carla suddenly lurched from her seat. Her fishing rod was bowing, bobbing and yanking in her tiny hands. Bob quickly grabbed hold to help her. Reeling as rapidly as possible, these two pulled in a hefty twelve-inch walleye. Carla was delighted with her whopping first catch.

Forgetting about the tranquillity of our boating expedition, we paddled excitedly to shore — talking, laughing and reliving the entire experience. We scrambled from the boat and hung the fish next to Carla since it was far too heavy for the tot to hold while we snapped pictures. After cleaning the walleye we had a party serving Carla's first catch, which had been fried over an open fire.

In everything give thanks: for this is the will of God in Christ Jesus.
~ 1 Thessalonians 5:18 KJV ~

Make Believe Mothering

*Instead of feeling overwrought with demands to the point of being
overwhelmed, feel the overflowing joy that comes from daily
life in the midst of a hustling, bustling family. The two halves
make one marvelous whole of God's balance.*

Each fall when school began, Carla and Rachel waved their
goodbyes and headed to the other side of the lake to the Christian
school. I sent them off and then turned my attention to Christa. We
packed the table, chairs and dishes along with dollies, a high chair and
baby bed together and with arms loaded down, we moved her items
from their usual home in her bedroom to a corner in the living room.
This way my toddler's playtime homemaking hours could be close by
her mother's real homemaking work.

The end table by the couch turned into a kitchen cupboard with
tiny plates, cups and doll bottles neatly lining the shelf. Christa's tiny
blender whirred up real chocolate milk. With one baby in the high chair,
one who was old enough to sit on a real chair and Christa perched on
the other, the trio would have one party after another. At times she lined
all the dolls up on the couch and collected a variety of books. For an
hour this pretend mommy had story time with her young ones.

Day after day, year after year, Christa enjoyed this kind of
mothering play. Those were precious times of watching my little one do
make-believe grown-up kinds of things. And could it be, I wondered,
that one day these training hours will pay off in enjoyable real
mothering?

*For I have set you an example.
~ John 13:15 ~*

Student of the Word

"Give Me thy heart," says the Father above,
No gift so precious to Him as our love;
Softly He whispers, wherever thou art,
"Gratefully trust Me, and give Me thy heart."
~ *Eliza E. Hewitt, 1851 - 1920* ~

Three-year-old Carla was forever busy with studies. Some days she'd be propped on a step poring over a magazine much beyond her mental abilities. Often, with pen and paper she wrote long detailed notes. Each line was completely full of scribbles that meant something, some item she had gleaned from her vigorous searching. Many times she could be found in her little rocking chair with her feet resting on an upside down laundry basket. Her shoulders were humped forward and her face down, buried in a book. Sometimes she jotted notes while other times she "read" her most intelligent make-believe story out loud.

How often I asked the Lord to guide Carla as she grew older to be this kind of student of the Word. My longings for this tiny girl when grown up would be that she search the mind of Christ, call on His name and jot notations of His messages in devotional journals. In my heart I knew not one of my prayers would be wasted.

I want to know Christ.
~ Philippians 3:10 ~

Emergency Landing

*My job is to take care of the possible and
trust God with the impossible.*
~ Ruth Bell Graham ~

While living in northern Ontario, Bob and his pilot were enroute in a tiny aircraft to their place of meeting. Four-year-old Rachel was accompanying her father on this particular trip and she contentedly sat or slept in the back of the noisy plane as it flew along.

At home, I was reading a story to Christa, who was a little over a year old. Around 3:15 pm I sensed in my heart a need to pray for the travelers. I paused from my reading and said to Christa, "I think we should pray for daddy and Rachel." She suggested, " No, read." I proceeded to read a few more sentences and then said, "No Christa, I think Jesus wants us to pray for Daddy right now." Huddled together, the two of us called on the name of the Lord. I didn't know the reason the Spirit was prompting me to pray, so I simply asked for safety, protection and blessing for everyone in the airplane. Once finished, we continued with our story.

Several hours later, we received a phone call reporting that everyone was fine, but the plane had gone down on a large lake. The floatplane had been uneventfully flying over miles of thick, dense bush for quite some time. Just as it approached a lake there was a very loud bang, then all was quiet and the propeller stood stark still. This happened at 3:15 pm, the very moment the Lord had impressed on me to stop reading and pray.

The small aircraft began an immediate downward descent; however, the pilot was able to glide the plane towards the water. Rachel, who had been asleep, was promptly awakened with the loud noise. As the plane continued its rapid decline toward the water below, Rachel's father kept encouraging her to relax and pray. Everyone in the plane sighed in relief upon the safe water landing and gave thanks to the Lord for His protection. Would this had happened mintues before, there would have been no water for safe landing and the plane would have gone down in the forest.

The two men crawled out of the plane and began to inspect the engine, quickly finding the problem. A rod had gone through the cylinder; however, there was nothing these men could do to remedy the situation this far from civilization. At the opposite end of the lake there was a small village where one lone household resided year around. The task at hand was to get a radio message to the right person in order to get it on to that village resident.

For some time the pilot and Bob called an SOS message on the aircraft's two-way radio, again and again making the call. After a period of time with no response, the team hauled out the emergency kit from the back of the plane and set out to start a fire. Rachel was left in the bobbing airplane, which had been paddled to shore and tied to a tree. She was snug and warm, tightly wrapped in sleeping bags. Her job was to listen intently to the radio in case a response came in from someone who may have heard the plea for help.

Hours went by and the battery in the plane was waning and needed to be shut down. The men carefully carried Rachel along the plane's float to the warm fire where soup was heating in a kettle. It was a mystery as to how long they might be stranded at their temporary campsite, but all three knew the Lord was with them wherever they were. Thus, they had a grand time camping and fellowshiping together.

Just about dark, the trio perked up their ears. It seemed the hushed stillness of this silent country was being broken by something. Straining their ears to hear and piercing their eyes to see, they listened and watched with purpose. They thought they heard a motor! Faraway in the distance, the three could slightly make out the outline of a boat. This group nearly shouted their excitement as the boat came closer and closer.

Aboard the boat was an older man who spoke no English. He was so thankful to have found the stranded ones and they were overjoyed to see him. Bob, Rachel and the pilot celebrated and gave thanks to the Lord for His provision.

The plane was tied to the boat and the pilot crawled in to steer it while Bob and Rachel stepped aboard and slowly started towards the rescuer's cabin. Once there, the men radioed the nearest town and learned that a jet pilot flying somewhere high overhead had heard their SOS message and successfully relayed the call to the appropriate person. For some reason, their rescuer had turned his radio on for a short period of time early that evening and received the message about the three in need.

Three days of bad weather set in causing the crew to remain stranded with the villagers since there was no possibility of a mechanic flying in to assist with the plane's trouble or to take the abandoned ones home. Bob, Rachel and the pilot were able to enjoy sweet fellowship with the villagers as they all served the same Lord and had that common bond.

Young Rachel was not used to eating off the land and she found it hard to partake of the beaver meat that was cheerfully cooked for the unexpected guests. Somehow the fish was just as unappealing to her. Her lack of eating concerned their elderly host, so two days into their stay, he pulled out a box of canned goods that he had purchased when he had been out to a town. He studied the contents and settled on some food that he believed Rachel might like. He was right. As she ate a whole can of blueberry pie filling, the older gentleman excitedly motioned to the men his thankfulness that the little girl was at last eating food.

On the third day of their expedition, the group was happy to see the bad weather lift. Early in the morning a plane was heard flying overhead, circling the tiny village of log cabins before making a smooth, pleasant landing right out front of the villagers' home. Bidding their kind friends goodbye, the three made their way to the plane and headed for home, taking with them a treasure chest full of new, fond memories and special friends. ✒

In my distress I called to the Lord;
My cry came before Him, into His ears.
~ Psalm 18:6 ~

It May Not be on the Mountain's Height

Mary Brown

It may not be on the mountain's height,
Or over the stormy sea;
It may not be at the battle's front
My Lord will have need of me.
But if, by a still small voice,
He calls to paths that I do not know,
I'll answer, dear Lord with my hand in Thine,
I'll go where you want me to go.

(Chorus)
I'll go where you want me to go, dear Lord,
Over mountain, or plain, or sea;
I'll say what you want me to say, dear Lord,
I'll be what you want me to be.

Perhaps today there are loving words
Which Jesus would have me speak;
There may be now in the paths of sin
Some wanderer whom I should seek;
O Savior, if Thou wilt be my guide,
Though dark and rugged the way,
My voice shall echo Thy message sweet,
I'll say what you want me to say.

There's surely somewhere a lowly place,
In earth's harvest fields so wide,
Where I may labor thro' life's short day
For Jesus, the Crucified;
So trusting my all to Thy tender care,
And knowing Thou lovest me,
I'll do Thy will with a heart sincere,
I'll be what you want me to be.

Section Two

Growing Up

And Jesus grew in wisdom and stature,
and in favor with God and men.
~ Luke 2:52 ~

WINTER WOOD PILES

Every job is a self-portrait of the person who does it.
Autograph your work with excellence.

The long winter evenings in our northern home were a quiet part of our family life. They kept the pace of our lives slowed as we cozied together around toasty fires to keep snug, warm and to simply enjoy. These fires of course, had to be fueled with wood and it took lots of wood for the many months of minus zero degree weather.

Each Saturday our three young daughters bundled as warm as they could and joined their father out at the woodpile. One by one the split and dried logs needed to be loosened from the ice and snow. Each piece was thrown into the wheelbarrow or on to the toboggan. It took a host of ready hands to make the work light, easy and rapid in this frigid weather.

Every wheelbarrow load was pushed across the drifts of snow to the frosty basement window. The window was pried open and the wood handed inside piece by piece to the waiting hands that stacked it in a row as high as the ceiling. Some hours later, with everyone invigorated and worn, each made their way back into the ever-warm house to the awaiting hot chocolate.

Seven short days later, the little tribe was back out at the same woodpile. The same hard work was repeated once again and each Saturday after that for many long months.

These Saturday wood working days held many a lesson for these growing girls; they found the hard work could actually be enjoyable and fortifying, plus it never paid to complain. The three certainly enjoyed the rewards of the great times with dad, a delightfully warm house and the hot chocolate that never tasted better. ✍

Whatever your hand finds to do, do it with all your might.
~ Ecclesiastes 9:10a ~

42

Snowmobile Train

A good deed is never lost; he who shows courtesy reaps friendship,
and he who plants kindness gathers love.
~ St. Basil ~

Snowmobiling fun was endless in the severely cold winter
months in the north. Carla, 11, called her sisters, Rachel, 10, and Christa,
7, into the party. Warm cloaks — from hats to boots — were yanked from
the closet and zipped into place.

Tying a toboggan tight to the snow machine, the trio started off.
Amidst the thick bush around our house were five other homes in a
large circular drive. These girls would stop at each home and collect
passengers. As one family group pulled on snowsuits and mitts, the
ringleaders would slide to the next home to alert them of the upcoming
snowmobile train. Moms hauled out the smaller children and tucked
them between the legs of older ones, and the parade moved on. When the
toboggan got full, bright colored plastic sleds were wired securely
behind. Around and around the circle this band of children slid.

About thirty minutes later, refreshed and vitalized, each child
was dropped off at their front door. The bundling and unbundling,
hanging wet mitts by the fire and lining boots in neat order was worth
every moment of energy for these busy moms. Being a part of the
snomobile train on an icy cold day meant heaps to each little tot.

The Lord will satisfy your needs.
~ Isaiah 58:11 ~

43

Snuffles the Hamster

Customs and traditions help define us and give uour family its identyty.

Pets were a trial at our house, which was full of little girls. We always wanted pets, but for the most part, once we had them, we didn't enjoy the little creatures. They often looked sad and lonely as we neglected their need to play. However, 6-year-old Rachel perceived that a hamster would be one breathing animal that we would all enjoy.

Believe it or not, a hamster was purchased along with all the proper items to keep him contented and satisfied. Since he was forever snuffling his nostrils, he was promptly named the most fitting and creative of all names — Snuffles.

Snuffles did enjoy some fun times at our little bungalow. He would quiet down when we pet him and sit bolt upright on the sofa next to his proud owner. He also kept our little girls quite entertained by spinning the wheel in his cage ever so quickly.

Snuffles caused us some adventure also. Somehow, he managed to get out of the door of his home one day and was nowhere to be found. A large area in the back of the couch that had been chewed full of holes was evidence enough that he was in the house, but we could not find the little critter anywhere. A few days later, looking blurry eyed and guilty, he was found under a bed, captured from any more trouble.

We awoke one morning a few days after Snuffles had been safely returned to his cage to find the telephone wasn't working. The repairman was called and his search outside the house turned up nothing. But upon looking inside the house, he solved the mystery rather quickly. Snuffles had chewed a hole completely through the phone cord.

Snuffles stayed with us a little while longer, but true to the nature of our family, he lost his glamour just as the other pets that once belonged there had. Another home was found for our adventurous friend and we settled back into life as a house full of little girls. 🐾

God made... all the creatures that move along
the ground according to their kinds.
~ Genesis 1:25b ~

Birthday Blessings

Kind words can be short and easy to speak but their echoes are truly endless.
~ Mother Teresa ~

It was my birthday and I needed to be away for the day. This gave my growing young daughters a perfect opportunity to test their limited kitchen skills. Unknown to me, they pulled out cookbooks and studied recipes until they fancied upon just the right ones — a lush, chocolate cake and perfect butter cream icing.

On that is particular day, these responsible girls, ages 5, 8 and 9, were caring for some neighbor children several years younger than they. Six children under nine in the kitchen seemed to create enthusiasm, and they set to work.

The batter was mixed and the cake was baked. Before it was finished baby Kieth needed a nap so he was rocked and tucked into bed. With that accomplished the five young ones continued at their task. Cleaning up the cake preparations seemed endless, but when finished, it was time to mix the icing together. The kitchen was turned upside-down once again. However, the children found it well worth the mess when they partook of the first lick of frosting. The girls filled the rarely used cake decorating set with the icing. How they marveled at the feel of the frosting as it was squeezed out of the tube across their tongues. It was so superb that indeed it was important for the baby to enjoy this privilege as well. The young caregivers knew babies prefer to not be wakened during their naps, but awakened he was. Too young for a taste, he got one anyway, along with another and another. If nothing else, the slick squish into his mouth hushed him for a few seconds from his overtired state, and the work continued.

The cake was precisely covered with the leftover icing. It looked faultless after great lengths of smoothing, licking, re-smoothing and re-licking. Carla, the leader of this time-consuming project, found many ways to use the cake decorator and create designs all across the top. Each person was allowed their turn to add the decor of their choice until the cake was perfectly completed. Standing back, this young group marveled at their prize.

Minutes later Naomi, the mother of the three small children, arrived to collect her family. Eagerly talking at once, everyone told of their day together as Christa picked up the cake to give Naomi a closer look. Suddenly, the cake that had taken so many hours to prepare and had filled this home with such entertainment, flipped from young Christa's hands. It landed face down on the kitchen floor. Everyone became breathlessly silent. Dear Christa felt sorely distressed and was just ready to burst into tears when her sister Carla said, "That's okay Christa, we can fix it." With Naomi's help, the team cleaned up the floor and worked diligently on the cake until it looked just fine.

By the time I arrived home everything was calm. I was delightfully surprised with this wonderful birthday treasure. Upon hearing the entire story, my heart was most thrilled at the gentle way Carla had cared for her younger sister. A different response could have meant a very disheartening end to such a grand day. "That's okay Christa, we can fix it." I felt like perhaps we were on our way to making this verse come true:

Be kind and compassionate to one another, forgiving each other,
just as in Christ God forgave you.
~ Ephesians 4:32 ~

Puzzle Time

I have a mother, I'm glad to say;
Who shares her love, all through the day.
I have a father, I'm glad to say;
Who shows his love, day after day.
I have two sisters, they love me too.
Our love is special, the whole year through.
With God we make six, He joins us too.
Love is unending, a circle tis' true.
~ Christa Kauffman Schwartz (age 8) ~

Sunday afternoons in our house were great times for doing quiet family activities. On many of those days we pulled out the folding table and filled it full with puzzles. One by one we dumped puzzles out and put them back together.

As the girls grew older we switched to jigsaw puzzles. The table was left sitting in the living room through the long winter months while one puzzle and then the next was carefully pieced together. There were scenery puzzles, pet pictures and picnic scenes. Once finished, it was not an easy task to tear those beautiful portraits apart. Consequently, with puzzles lying here and there, we purchased puzzle glue, cemented each one together and decorated our basement wall with them.

Puzzle time gave opportunities for sharing our hearts in a peaceful manner when two or three of us crowded around the table at once. At times, one of us worked alone and used those moments to think, meditate and reflect. We found there was something about working on puzzles that quieted our spirits no matter what our age. The basement wall that contained every size, shape and color of puzzles held a ring of memories we'll cherish forever. 🍃

Let the peace of Christ rule in your hearts.
~ Colossians 3:15 ~

Love at Home

John H. McNaughton, 1829-1896

There is beauty all around, When there's love at home;
There is joy in every sound, When there's love at home;
Peace and plenty here abide, Smiling sweet on every side,
Time doth softly, sweetly glide, When there's love at home,
Love at home, love at home;

Time doth softly, sweetly glide, When there's love at home.
In the cottage there is joy, When there's love at home;
Hate and envy ne'er annoy, When there's love at home;
Roses blossom 'neath our feet, All the earth's a garden sweet,
Making life a bliss complete, When there's love at home,
Love at home, love at home;

Making life a bliss complete, When there's love at home.
Kindly heaven smiles above, When there's love at home;
All the earth is filled with love, When there's love at home;
Sweeter sings the brooklet by, Brighter beams the azure sky;
Oh, there's One who smiles on high When there's love at home,
Love at home, love at home,

Oh, there's One who smiles on high, When there's love at home.
Jesus, show Thy mercy mine, Then there's love at home;
Sweetly whisper "I am thing," Then there's love at home;
Source of love, Thy Cheering light Far exceeds the sun so bright —
Can dispel the gloom of night, Then there's love at home,
Love at home, love at home.

Best Friends

A genuine friendship is a heavenly present.
It blesses our hearts because God is in it.
~ Evelyn McCurdy ~

Carla and Mary's friendship started when they were just toddlers. The two of them spent hours and years of innocent delightful play together. Blissful summer days were spent in the lake or building sandcastles. Canoeing and camping in a bushy hollow brought thrills and shrieks of excitement that wafted into the house.

On deep blue fall days, these girls found their haven in the attic where they sorted through boxes and bags. They organized and built little homes for each one in private corners then mothered and cooed over their doll babies.

The quiet, snowy winter months found this inseparable pair in their clubhouse. It was in this clubhouse that blessed new heights came into view. These were the beginning days of each learning the quiet of their own personal devotional time with the Lord. Next it was together times in the Word. Special notes were written to important people while huddled together in the three-by-three-foot walls built by Mary's father for this important club. Goals were established here and dreams jotted down. Giggles and laughter drifted from those thin paneled walls. Whispers of personal, private secrets were nearly audible.

As the years have come and gone, these two have wandered apart in the physical sense, but in heart and spirit, one could only describe their friendship as kindred spirits. Thus, the song they often sang continues to ring true:

Friends are Friends forever
If the Lord's the Lord of them...
...and a lifetime's not to long to live as friends.

Thank the Lord for His steadfast love and for
His wonderful works to humankind.
~ Psalm 107:8 ~

Funnel Cakes

Some people come into our lives and quickly go ...
Some stay for awhile and leave footprints on our hearts,
and we are never the same.
~ Unknown ~

One fall evening Carla, 14, and Rachel, 13, invited their friend April for a visit. Contemplating the best way to spend the evening, the three girls decided upon making funnel cakes. They found the right recipe and set to work.

The gooey dough was mixed together to a perfect consistency for slowly running through a funnel. Oil was heated to just the right temperature in an electric frying pan.

The fun began when the trio worked to pour the dough through the funnel and weave that utensil around just above the hot oil to make artistic-looking shapes. Taking turns, they toiled over drawing the first initial of their names. Almost before they got the shape formed, the browning cake needed to be flipped. In the process of turning it over, the creation fell apart. While one fished the strange looking fried thing from the pan, another quickly sprinkled powdered sugar over it and carried it off to one of the family to enjoy. Next they worked to shape a heart and then a circle, though nothing seemed to stay in place during the entire process. At last imaginative designs were laid aside and simple globs that held together nicely were fried quickly, removed, sprinkled with sugar and passed around.

The funnel cakes were a delicious treat that evening, but the most enjoyable part of the whole party was observing these girls so diligently at work. Making decisions, cleaning up messes, sharing ideas, being creative and accomplishing the undertaking. If you would like to enjoy this experience for yourselves, mix together a recipe for thin pancakes and make your own funnel cakes. 𝒟

He will yet fill your mouth with laughter and your lips with shouts of joy.
~ Job 8:2 ~

Snowball Fight

Laughter is the language of the young at heart. And you know what?
You don't have to be happy to laugh. You become happy because you laugh.
~ Barbara Johnson ~

It was pushing spring after the long icy winter months. School was closed for the day but we parents felt comfortable leaving our teens to care for their younger siblings while we attended a meeting.

The young folks that lived on the south side of the lake had chatted with the ones on the north side and made plans to get together for some fun. Snowmobiles were revved up and then raced across the lake. The snow packed great and the fun began as forts were built and snowballs began flying. This activity was taking place at our house and soon someone happened into the kitchen door with snowballs following. This created an even greater enthusiasm amongst the snow-covered teens.

About this same time, our meeting adjourned and we parents headed home. As Bob and I drove into our drive, snowballs appeared to stop in midair and children scattered. What a sight I saw as I came through the kitchen door! Dotted around the room were girls soaking wet from their heads to their feet. The kitchen floor was under what seemed like an inch of melted snowballs with clumps of leftover balls continuing to add more liquid to the enormous puddle. Carla looked rather uncomfortable as she stood there wondering what my response might be. Her outer clothes were dripping and strands of hair hung in wet ringlets around her youthful, fun-filled face.

We marveled at the good-natured fun this day had brought. The kitchen floor was cleaned up rapidly, drenched children and clothing were quickly dried and barrels of joyful chatter filled our home throughout the evening. The memory lingers in the hearts of these youth, now responsible adults and parents, who took literally the encouragement of the following verse:

This is the day the LORD has made; let us rejoice and be glad in it.
~ Psalm 118:24 ~

A Touch of the Lord

The most important prayer in the world
is just two words long: "Thank you."
~ Meister Eckhart ~

Towards the close of a trip focusing on parenting seminars to Northwest Territories, we had one last stop in northern Manitoba where we planned to have a few services, which included singing together as a family. While at this last stop, 9-year-old Carla took sick early one morning. We were far from home and the care of our doctors. We collected our little family and gathered at her bedside where we laid hands on her and sought the Lord to reach down and touch her weakened body with health and strength. We claimed the promise of Acts 28:8 KJV, "Paul entered in, and prayed, and laid hands on him, and healed him."

We quietly left her to rest for several more hours and then, just minutes before the first service was to begin, Carla got up and declared she was well. She prepared herself and was able to join us for each service at this Inuit community.

Over the years, our girls traveled and ministered with us wherever we went. We experienced many answers to prayer that taught these little ones about the God we serve. On many occasions, we collected together to offer our thanks to the Lord for another miracle, just as we did again this time before we left for the first service.

With thanksgiving, let your requests be made known unto God.
~ Philippians 4:6 KJV ~

I'M A SHEEP

I see homeschooling through rosy-colored glasses
as it is one of my favorite pastimes;
~ Sharon Kuepfer ~
(Home schooling Tips and Child-Friendly Recipes)

We were invited to join a group of home school families and excitedly planned for our children to work together in preparing and performing a play. The little drama called for intense effort on everyone's part, so we families met together regularly. Dad's gave encouragement and guidance to each child as they diligently practiced and memorized lines. Mom's sat together sharing the joys and trials in this most noble feat of child rearing.

Hours of hard work and weeks later, the night arrived for our children to share their delightful "We Like Sheep" performance. I carefully painted 10-year-old Christa's nose pitch black to perfectly match the rest of the actors. Each child was garbed in white and had two floppy ears much like that of real, wooly sheep. Friends, grandparents and other relatives came together to enjoy this special evening. In such a pleasant manner these children portrayed the blessed story of Christ the gentle Shepherd and we His sheep, so hopeless without His ever-guiding hand. The never-ending practices, persistence in memorizing, splendid success and the pitch black noses made everything all worth the while. ✎

I am the good shepherd: the good shepherd giveth his life for His sheep.
~ John 10:11 ~

Prison Ministry

Work is love made visible.
~ Kalil Gibran ~
(The Prophet)

Our house full of ladies meant that the housework was quickly completed. Breaks between home schooling academic periods worked perfectly for getting laundry hung on the clothesline, dusting or cleaning a bathroom. This freed our afternoons for extracurricular activities. Christa, 14, invited two of her home school friends to join her in spending one afternoon each week volunteering at a local prison ministry office. The girls never knew what those volunteer hours might bring.

Their limited typing skills were stretched and they learned all about following instructions carefully, working on courtesy and other relational skills. The trio addressed and stuffed envelopes and collated stacks of papers. Prison inmates earned a Bible upon completion of a certain amount of Bible lessons, which meant that some afternoons the girls neatly wrote the name of each recipient in their new Bible, then packaged each one for mailing.

I knew my weekly efforts to round up the girls and deliver them for a few hours of ministry time were greatly rewarded as I listened to young Christa share heartfelt concern and burden for children with troubled parents. More than once she came to me in tears over a hurting soul. We'd pray together and deliberately decide to leave the child in the Lord's capable hands. My heart thrilled with the rewards from this kind of heart-stretching activities.

I was in prison, and you came to visit me.
~ Matthew 25:36 ~

Amazing Mother

My wheelchair has shown me that the path of holiness is not an easy journey ... but it's the right — no, the righteous — one.
~ Joni Eareckson Tada ~
(Holiness in Hidden Places)

Meeting at the kitchen table at 9:00 each morning gave us a good start to our home school day. During that hour, we read some kind of literature concerning Christian Heroes or mentors. One particular period of time we were reading books by Joni Eareckson Tada and studying the world of quadriplegics. Carla, 16, Rachel, 15, and Christa, 12, found this a fascinating study.

I recalled a time when I was a child when a family from my church had a tragic car accident leaving their fourteen-month-old daughter, Rhoda, paralyzed as a quadriplegic. The family had moved from our community when Rhoda was 3 years old and now many years had passed. I hadn't seen her since their move, but I learned she was recently married, had a child and was living in the same community as I was.

I phoned Rhoda and asked if I might bring my daughters for an interview to complete our study in the area and she wholeheartedly invited us for a visit. Rhoda showed us the little bed her husband, Ken had made which hung over their own bed. Its purpose was that she be able to get the baby to herself for nighttime nursing without waking her husband for each feeding. She was able to sit up by herself and maneuver the baby into her bed for this purpose.

Ken had also designed a crib that she could roll her wheelchair up to like a desk. With it being desk height, it was much easier for Rhoda to lift the baby on and off her lap into the crib, which served as a dressing table as well as sleeping quarters. The front side of the crib, easily slid up and over the top so it was out of the way while caring for the baby's needs. One side of the crib had three drawers that held essentials for Kiva while the other side had a rod that pulled out for hanging little dresses, making everything within Rhoda's reach. Diapers and clothing had been prepared with Velcro closures and worked rather smoothly for this young mother. Potty training was done in the crib as well. Rhoda could roll to the crib with her toddler and tend to her potty training needs at this height. Kiva learned at a young age that to get from the floor to her mother's lap she needed to crawl onto her mother's foot rests or to the side of the wheelchair, then with Rhoda's help, she could climb into her mother's lap for cuddling or soothing.

Several years prior to Kiva's birth, Rhoda had a surgical procedure done to her fingers that, she said, "Changed my life." Before the operation, she had no pinch at all. After the surgery, she could move each finger in a pinch position to her thumb. Her fingers did not grasp or clutch before, so this extra use was most essential in giving the needed care to her baby. Because of this surgery, Rhoda could zip a zipper that had been fixed with a pull on it and was also able to tie a shoe, though it didn't come quickly and easily to her. As Rhoda would tie Kiva's shoes she would teach each step again and again. Much to Rhoda's relief, Kiva learned to tie her own shoes while very young.

Our day with Rhoda and her family was most thought provoking and encouraging. We enjoyed learning, observing and sharing with these kind people. We were awed to discover first hand what a quadriplegic person faces and it was rewarding to enjoy Rhoda's spirit and acceptance. She was a living example of one who has learned to enjoy quietness and rest in our Lord amidst her trial-some situation. We didn't witness one negative word or attitude and went home from our hands-on study with renewed urgency to choose contentment and acceptance with our lot in life! ⅔

You have assigned me my portion and my lot, and made my lot secure.
~ Psalms 16:5 ~

(In a recent phone call with Rhoda, she informed me that she now has two daughters. Kiva is 13 years old, and her sister is 8. A friend, who also uses a wheelchair, lives with the family and provides home schooling for the girls.)

First Night in Foster Care

Happy is the home that shelters a friend.
~ *Ralph Waldo Emerson* ~

It was late in the evening when I returned from the hospital with Darrin, a 2 year old special-needs child. Carla, 16, Rachel, 15, and Christa, 12, had spent the day at home busily working on academics, laundry and routine housework.

Darrin had Dandy Walker Malformation of the Cerebellum, which left him with severe disabilities. We frequently provided respite care for him or his sister Stephanie, who was also diagnosed with the disease. Darrin had been in our care for a few days and was not feeling well. Thus, I had made the trip to the hospital where these siblings received their medical treatment.

We had recently signed up with an adoption agency to foster newborn babies awaiting placement in their adoptive homes. With three growing daughters that loved children and some available time for ministering, we opted for this plan. On this particular day, while I was three hours away with Darrin, the girls got a phone call. Carla answered the phone and the caller said, "This is Sara from the adoption agency." Carla was about ecstatic with the assumption that this call was about a baby, yet she was concerned because I was not home. Relaying this information, Sara responded, "Oh Carla that's fine, you girls know how to care for these tiny ones. I'll have the baby there at 4:00."

The house and school work were scrapped and immediate attention was turned to preparations for baby Matthew's arrival. The girls sorted through the storage boxes until the bassinet surfaced. It was hauled out, dusted off and prepared with soft sheets. They called Bob at his office to explain the latest happenings; he too was excited and could hardly wait to get home. The girls jumped into their little blue car, which had been purchased with baby-sitting money, and raced off to their aunt's house to retrieve any little boy clothes that might work. They planned to have Aunt Mary come promptly after work at 5:00 pm just in case they would need an older person around.

The time finally came for Matthew to arrive. With everything, ready and waiting, including the three girls, they peered out the window as Sara came bounding in with the baby as excited as the girls were. Under the little blanket lay the tiniest, sweetest, little guy they could ever imagine.

The girls had done a lot of childcare, but it seemed they had forgotten how fragile newborns were. This was such an exciting adventure and Matthew was tinier than they ever remembered seeing a baby, so Aunt Mary's presence provided some comfortable security. As soon as their dad arrived home everyone piled in the car and stopped to show Matthew to all the relatives in the whole community.

When I got home with our unhealthy little guy, I was weary and exhausted. I had driven a total of six hours, not to mention the hours of waiting in the emergency room concerned about what was troubling Darrin. I had hardly gotten one foot out of the car when this pack of people came rushing from the house with Christa joyfully toting the baby. I was excited as well, but so ready to stumble into bed for a long night of sleep!

Some hours later we got exhausted Darrin tucked in to the playpen in our bedroom. The apnea monitor was fixed in place, feeding tube hooked up properly and the little guy finally fell asleep. We snuggled Matthew in the bassinet just outside the girl's bedroom door after yet one more feeding with plans of the two older girls taking turns feeding him through the night. All seven of us fell into our inviting beds, which felt so good but no sleep came to us. Enthusiasm was so high that any possibility of sleep seemed to have disappeared.

After hours of tossing, turning and jumping at the stirrings of little ones plus feeding Matthew yet another time, everyone at last dozed off. Moments later, the alarming, sharp sound of Darrin's apnea monitor screamed in our ears. Bob bounded out of bed right with me and we scrambled to Darrin's side just as the loud screech of the machine roused him back to breath! Of course the lightly sleeping household had heard the blaring noise and all had joined us in desperation to be assured that Darrin was okay. Apprehensive about his condition, we laid hands on his small head and asked the Lord to protect him through the remainder of the night.

We pattered back to our beds and were quieting our hearts and minds when baby Matthew's crying plea came for one more bottle of formula. The young caregivers found it rather difficult to drag their worn bodies from their beds, but it was obvious there would be no silence until they did. Matthew didn't wish to settle easily, which called for some help from the wide-awake, exhausted mother. Some long two hours later, the sweet one was peacefully tucked back in the bassinet. Each of us stole quietly to our beds in hopes of some desperately needed sleep. We all dozed for one short blissful hour when the apnea monitor again blasted its piercing scream. Everyone raced another time to Darrin's side, grateful, once again, that the alarm had alerted him back to good deep breaths. Choosing again to leave him in the Lord's hands, saddened over his condition and weak from our loss of sleep, we staggered to our beds.

Seconds later, at 5:00 am, Matthew frantically wailed out his need for more food. I started to chuckle as I crawled, rather fell, back out of my bed and staggered across the house to my daughters door where they were one more time pulling themselves to their feet. I flopped onto their bed laughing and told them, "I am not going back to bed. You crawl back in and go to sleep; I will feed the baby and get the day started."

So was our first night in foster care. With providing this kind of care came great rewards as we enjoyed the nine infants that came and went in our home. We hurt inside each time another left. While the deep loss was painful, we prayed over the dear ones and their birth mothers that had wanted the best for them. We met delight-filled adoptive parents and placed their baby into their arms. We sent the tiny ones off with pictures and a diary of their days with us. To our amazement and joy, baby Matthew was placed in a lovely home just minutes from ours. How thankful we were to visit the little boy who had became so important to us. 🦋

Suffer the little children to come unto me.
~ Mark 10:14 ~

(Young Darrin wasn't able to win his battle here on earth. He struggled through pain and suffering for six short years. He went to the Lord to receive His reward — a new body. It was a dark bleak day for his kind parents, friends and family, but we rejoice that Darrin is delighting in the presence of His loving heavenly Father.)

My Baby Alina

*Even as it is the nature of a seed to sprout, it
is the nature of love to give itself away.*
~ Robert Schuller ~
(Tough Times Never Last but Tough People Do)

We had packed her things the night before and crawled into bed with lumps in our throats. The next morning the little girl who had lived with us for the past eight months would leave; her father and grandmother would pick her up at 11:00 am.

Alina came to our home when she was 4-months-old. She moved deep into our hearts with her delightful and contended misdemeanor as she grew to completely love our house full of adults. Alina experienced her many firsts with us and we marveled at each new antic and praised her for every charming move. We could hardly fathom the joy this tiny one's presence brought to our house. Nor did we have any concept of the thick emptiness we would feel as her daddy drove her away the next morning, Friday, September 27, 1991. Pen and paper can not describe the pain in our souls as we four girls closed the door behind our tiny baby girl, sank into chairs and sobbed for ... we don't know how long.

There was no promise of ever seeing our little girl again. She had been so happy and so loved with us that we wondered what her new world would bring and if anyone would tell her the stories of Jesus. I snatched her smiling photos off the wall, as the ache was far too great to look at her joy-filled face. Giving her to someone else felt worse than death to me. Surely with Jesus, I knew her joy would be complete.

A week later, when our grief was still thicker than words can describe, some kind friends invited us out to dinner. On our way home, we stopped at a store to collect a few items. It was difficult for me to even go into a building filled with busy people oblivious to my desperate hurt. As we were wandering around, I caught a glimpse of someone and said to my friend, "Who is that?" We walked a little further down the aisle and there she was. "Alina," I shouted, "Alina!" Her daddy and his girlfriend turned around at Alina's shrill squeal and my loud outburst. Alina giggled and wiggled. Reaching out to grab my baby, not quite a year old, I remembered she was no longer *my* baby. I stopped my hands midair and asked her daddy if I could hold his little girl. I picked up the exuberant one and we cuddled, hugged and chuckled our delight.

All too soon, it was time to go and I had to give her back. I put her in the cart and turned to walk away. I turned to look back to see Alina watching me. We did just that, looked into each other's eyes until her daddy rolled the cart around a corner and she was gone. Gone, once again from my presence, but never from my heart.

Somehow, that short exchange quieted my aching arms and desperate longings for a few more days. I find this same thing happens between the Lord and me. We get so close when I consistently spend time with Him, daily drawing from His Word and His presence. And then, a busy time comes along that fills the space I would have normally used to sit at His feet. I become lonely and restless and in need of seeing the Master in a close way once again. Retrieving back that time restores me with a rest in my spirit—much like seeing Alina one week after she had left ministered quietness to my desperate mourning.

My presence will go with you and I will give you rest.
~ Exodus 33:14 ~

61

Best Birthday Ever

God can take your trouble
and change it into treasure
~ Barbara Johnson ~

It hadn't been quite a month since Alina had gone to live with her father and my days were still heavy and lonely. I wondered if the dull ache would ever go away; I missed my baby so.

Each day, the girls and I would try to start our home school day at the kitchen table, true to routine, but now it was so different. Remembering how Alina used to interrupt us with her delightful tricks, I'd end up in tears. Carla, Rachel and Christa, quietly dabbing at their eyes, would patter off to their desks and start schoolwork without our kitchen table routine.

As my birthday rolled around everyone in my family wondered what I'd like to do to make my day special. Somehow nothing seemed interesting to me. The deep ache in my heart hung over my head like a thick cloud.

Sadly, I sat the table for dinner on that sorrowful birthday evening. Just focusing on doing the next task at hand and working to survive the next hour and the next night. As Bob drove in from work, I happened to glance out the window and noticed there was someone in the car with him. I studied through the glass and there she was. It was Alina! Bob had invited Alina and her daddy for my birthday surprise. I raced out the door and grabbed my baby girl. My heart thumped with excitement and with apprehension, for I knew enjoying her again also meant sending her away yet another time.

I carried Alina into the house and we pulled out the lonely toys and dollies as she studied every room of the home she had been so familiar with. We doted over her, hugged and cuddled her all through the evening. Her little heart seemed so confused as she fussed unusually different than ever before. We did all we could to lavish the little one with security and love. All too soon, we packed her back up, held her close, prayed over her and sent her on her way one more time.

This has been the story of our lives since that day. Alina has come and gone many times over the last eleven years. She lives with her mother, step father and two half sisters. She's bigger now and busy with her own things so we don't see her as often as before, but we keep in touch. We can never describe the tender spot that she fills in our hearts. The lonely ache in my heart on my birthday eleven years ago has long since been replaced with fullness, as even Alina's mother and I have become cherished friends.

And they brought young children to him, that He should touch them.
~ Mark 10:13 ~

Innocent Angels

Each loving act says loud and clear, I love you. God loves you. I care. God cares.
~ *Joyce Heinrich and Anetta La Placa* ~

Our family provided respite care for several years to Jessica, a special needs little girl. Jessica isn't able to talk, but her endless, bubbling, silent smile makes her a delight.

The bus dropped Jessica off at our house each day at 4:00 pm from her day at school. Mary Ann, who was also a special needs child, sat in her wheelchair at the front of the big yellow vehicle and would see me as soon as I bounded up the steps to collect four-year-old Jessica. She'd lift her head, flap her little hands, and say in her broken way of speaking, "I - want - to - see - Jessica." Coming from the back of the bus with Jessica in his arms, the driver would pause beside Mary Ann, and these little girls, in their own communicative manner would say a pleasant good bye to one another. This done, Jessica and I proceeded down the steps off the bus.

After a time Jessica changed schools, which meant she no longer rode the same bus as Mary Ann did. This also meant that I wasn't able to see Mary Ann either. Some months later as I was driving into church one Sunday morning, I saw Mary Ann's mother pushing her in her wheelchair for an early morning stroll. I jumped out of my car and raced to the sidewalk. I said, "Mary Ann, how are you?" Lifting her head she looked at me as I asked, "Do you remember Jessica?" A bright smile crossed her face as her mother responded, "Jessica! Oh, she misses Jessica." With that Mary Ann emphatically nodded her whole body in agreement and repeated, "Jess-i-ca."

These delightful special girls have a way of radiating sunshine from their hearts right into mine. The Lord uses extraordinary children to enrich my life with deeper compassion. Jessica took hours of special care, but her bubbling, quiet smile always touched me with a pleasant calm even on the days when my spirit was anything but calm.

He gathers the lambs in His arms and carries them close to His heart.
~ *Isaiah 40:11* ~

Jesus Calls the Children

C. H. Woolston

Jesus loves the little children,
All the children of the world.
Red and yellow, black and white,
All are precious in His sight,
Jesus loves the little children of the world.

(Chorus)
Jesus died for all the children,
All the children of the world.
Red and yellow, black and white,
All are precious in His sight,
Jesus died for all the children of the world.

Jesus is the Shepherd true,
And He'll always stand by you,
For He loves the little children of the world;
He's a Savior great and strong,
And He'll shield you from the wrong,
For He loves the little children of the world.

I am coming, Lord, to Thee,
And Your soldier I will be,
For You love the little children of the world;
And Your cross I'll always bear,
And for You I'll do and dare,
For You love the little children of the world.

Section Three

Kindred Spirits

I have no greater joy than to hear that my children
are walking in the truth.

~ 3 John 4 ~

Grown-Up Daughters

She never quite leaves her children at home,
even when she doesn't take them along.
~ *Margaret Culkin Banning* ~
(Heart of Purest Gold)

It was six years that Rachel and her husband, Glen had waited for a child. Indeed, everyone was overjoyed with the miracle of Sierra's birth. Christa and husband, Rod, had little Kyle two years into their marriage. Our family of adults was just that for too many years, and we were ready for these little tots.

Along with the babies came some definite adjustments! Rachel and Glen were visiting the rest of us in Ohio from their home in Virginia. Kyle was 8 months old and Sierra had hit the four- month mark. The general rule over the years had been that the women take some time for shopping when Rachel came to visit; however, now we had babies and they were fussy. Kyle had an ear infection and Sierra was not at all sure of her unfamiliar relatives doting over her. With this in mind, I offered to keep the little ones while the girls went on the shopping expedition.

By now, Christa and Rachel were making the transition from wife to mother and life had changed for them. Preparing to leave, the two mamas had no jackets. It's much easier to just haul baby to the car neglecting the need for a coat for themselves. It was chilly and they wondered what to do, so I suggested they could each wear one of mine. In the past, they would have been concerned that the one looks like one their grandma wears and the other isn't much better; however, it seemed to not matter so much anymore. Christa said, "I'll wear the blue one," and Rachel pulled on the one that was gold.

Carla, the particular, single, eldest sister began to grow a bit concerned about this whole plan. In a sort of shock at the events that were taking place so quickly, she backed against the wall with an aghast look across her face— those jackets were rather questionable if her sisters were going to be with her!

The two young mothers also no longer carried purses. For Christmas they had each gotten the other a little wallet that fit nicely into their diaper bags. But now they didn't know what to do with no purses and no diaper bags. These wallets didn't seem handy for simply carrying on the shopping trip. Rachel thought she could stick one in each of the huge pockets on her old-fashioned coat and plopped them in there. Carla, coming out of her stunned state, fumbled for words, moaned, then stuttered, "No, girls, no. I have purses in my room that you can use." Christa quickly blurted out her solution, "Oh, I know, we'll just put the wallets in the stroller." With giggles, everyone remembered at once that there would be no stroller since the babies were staying with Grandma. With that, Carla promptly got purses for her two sisters.

These mothers suddenly remembered that the night before had been rather disturbed with the little ones. Now they thought they would surely be tired during this shopping expedition. Standing over the counter snickering, they each drank a glass of mountain dew with hopes that it would give some quick energy, then they bounded to the car.

The door slammed behind the trio and I mused over the blessing of my grown daughters. The changes from those important youthful years, to the quiet and infertile years of being wife, to my single daughter, Carla, to my new mama daughter's, Rachel, and Christa. I bowed my heart in praise for what each path of life's journey had given my girls and turned my attention back to the two tiny grandbabies. I had prayed so long for these babies and had waited anxiously to grandmother them both at the very same time. This was my first chance. ✒

Praise be to the Lord, for He showed His wonderful love to me.
~ Psalm 31:21 ~

Baking Bread with Babies

Who but your mother shares your moments of glory? Who else sees you at your weakest and most vulnerable and picks you up, helping you grow strong? Your mom believes in your dreams, even when they lie in tatters at your feet. She picks you up and helps you dream again.
~ Brenda Hunter and Holly Larson ~
(In the Company of Friends)

Early one morning Christa breathlessly declared, "Mom, you will not believe what all has taken place in the last few minutes." Curious to hear the story, I prompted her to continue. With two babies under 19 months, I never knew what her morning might bring.

Christa had started mixing a batch of bread bright and early, deciding she'd get that going first thing and then she would get herself and the babies dressed for the day. As the mixer whirred the first ingredients together, she found her flour bin was empty. She raced upstairs and pulled a skirt over top of her pajama shirt. She was flipping her hair into a quick twist when she heard a pounding sound from the living room, followed by shrieks of weeping. Pound, pound, pound came the sound again and the crying turned to wails. Racing to 7-month-old Kassie's side, Christa said to her son Kyle, "What did you do to the baby?" Kyle, twelve months older than his sister, stood by with an apprehensive expression that quickly changed to sobs. He realized he'd hurt Kassie and had troubled his mother once again.

As Christa continued to soothe desperate Kassie, suddenly she saw blood. With that, this distressed mama heightened her rebuke and demanded to Kyle, "What did you do to the baby?" Glancing around the room she spied the "hammer" — a welcome light that had been pulled from the windowsill. The broken bulb showed evidence of the blood. By now, the whole household was in frantic tears. Mama was studying the tiny cuts on baby's hand. Still broken hearted, Kyle stealthily wandered to his mother and nestled down in her lap. He cuddled his tiny head against his mama and baby. Christa knew that deep down in Kyle's heart, he didn't want to hurt his sister. She also knew in the depths of her soul she didn't want to bruise Kyle's tender spirit. Snuggled together the trio forgave one another, comforted each other, wiped up blood spots and finally dried tears from six blurry eyes.

Suddenly remembering the bread, Christa picked her children up from the floor, bundled Kyle in his jacket and decided against Kassie's warm snowsuit, swaddling the baby in a thick blanket instead. She hauled the little family to the van and drove straight across the street to the grocery store. Still feeling frazzled, Christa wondered just how she was going to manage to get both children into the store. How could she keep the blanket tightly around the baby with Kyle in the other arm? It all appeared bigger than anything workable at the moment, so she made a hasty decision, one that she always talks herself out of. "I'll leave the baby in the van while I run in for one minute to get the bread flour," she thought.

Shutting the door behind her, Christa suddenly gasped, "I can't leave her in there, I can't." She turned around rapidly to open the door and ... it was locked! Frantic, she and Kyle raced into the little town store and begged the friendly clerk to watch her baby while she ran home to get another set of keys. Eager to help, the storekeeper followed Christa out the door. Racing to the house and back with Kyle in her arms had her all out of breath as she arrived back at the van. Two cashiers, along with two maintenance men stood guard at the van door talking with the baby who smiled cheerfully out at them. With relief, she collected Kassie from the van and, with the help of everyone gathered around, got her little tribe into an awaiting cart. Christa began to explain that she was making bread and had run out of flour. Since she had decided to mix the bread before baths, they were all still in pajamas, but, she explained to them, she would get them all bathed and dressed as soon as her bread was rising. She declared to me, "Oh Mom, I don't even know what all I said. I just got my flour and got out of there as fast as I could."

As she was paying for the flour, the kind cashier was exclaiming over what a wonderful little mother Christa was to be staying at home and baking bread with her children. She recalled days when she had done the same.

Once quietly secured back at the house, Christa thought, "I'll take some cookies over to those dear people. They were so helpful." However, as quickly as that idea fluttered in, it was discarded with the memories of taking two tiny tots to the store just moments earlier.

As Christa finished her long story, she chided herself for getting panicked and distraught. She didn't know why she felt so of control. "It's something I've really been working on," she confided, "I don't want to be one that panics."

How I recalled those days. They had come and gone as quickly as these precious mothering years would for Christa. Taking each one as they came, reprimanding and training, struggling through panics and impatience were a daily piece of living for me. And just as little Kyle, in his tiny one-year-old way sought forgiveness from mommy and baby, so did I on many an impatient and trouble-struck day.

As a mother comforts her child, so will I comfort you.
~ Isaiah 66:13 ~

Motherhood

E. L. Shirreff, 1897

Gracious Saviour, who didst honor
Woman kind as woman's Son;
Very Man, tho' God begotten,
And with God the Father one;
Grant our womanhood may be
Consecrated, Lord, to Thee.

Jesus, Son of human mother,
Bless our motherhood, we pray'
Give us grace to lead our children,
Draw them to Thee day by day;
May our sons and daughters be
Dedicated, Lord, to Thee.

Thou who didst with Joseph labor,
Nor didst humble work disdain,
Grant we may Thy footsteps follow
Patiently thro' toil or pain;
May our quiet home life be
Lived, O Lord, in Thee, to Thee.

Thou who didst go forth in sorrow,
Toiling for the souls of men,
Thou who shalt draw all men to Thee,
Tho' despised, rejected then;
Humble tho' our influence be,
Use it in the world for Thee.

Cinnamon Roll Creation

Celebrate the happiness that friends are always giving,
making every day a holiday and celebrate just living.
~ Amanda Bradley ~

Carla came up from her apartment in our basement and said, "The girls would like to make cinnamon rolls." That sounded like a grand plan to me, for I had just mixed up a recipe and a half and the dough was rising in a large bowl. I was thrilled to have Carla and her two visiting friends take over my project. I helped her collect everything needed to finish the project, dumped it all into another large bowl, and Carla balanced both containers in her hands as she meandered back down the steps to her waiting friends.

Not long into their new plan, I heard the holler for "mom." Wandering down to the basement, I wondered if these three single women had ever made cinnamon rolls before. It didn't take long to learn they didn't know what they were doing. "What do we do with these two containers full of stuff?" was their first question. Sprinkling flour on the five foot long counter and scraping the dough from the bowl, I explained to the girls that this huge hunk of sticky dough needed rolled into an 18- inch wide, three foot long, one-half inch thick piece. I detailed the rest of the directions and went back upstairs.

Fifteen minutes later the trio could not figure out how you would actually get the dough into a roll. I had explained to roll it width-wise; however, Sheila wanted to roll it tightly, Renee thought loosely and Carla was sure neither of those methods were right. I quickly illustrated how to roll it all up in a very long roll. With it all rolled together, it stretched to some four and one-half feet. I hadn't told the girls quite the size batch I was making and they had no clue by looking.

I proceeded to teach these girls how to stretch and cut the long roll in right width rounds and put them in the lightly greased tins. Renee took the pizza cutter in hand and began the slicing process. Carla took each delicate glob from the cutting board and laid it in the tin, and Sheila neatly shaped the awkward looking clumps into perfect cinnamon roll forms. Deciding the oven in the basement didn't work well enough to bake the rolls, Sheila was elected to carry all twelve pans of the rapidly rising buns up the steps. The other two beat the butter cream frosting together and cleaned up the sticky mess.

That extra large batch of cinnamon rolls turned out so light, fluffy and scrumptious that we ate two tins in just a few minutes. I'm thinking these young adults will remember how to make cinnamon rolls when they're 90 years old.

Following is the recipe for these delicious rolls and the frosting:

Cinnamon Rolls

2 cups scalded milk	1 cup sugar
2 cups warm water	1 tablesppon salt
4 tablespoons yeast	4 eggs, beaten
1/2 pound margarine	1 teaspoon nutmeg (optional)
9 - 10 cups flour	

Place yeast in bowl, add 2 cups warm water. Stir slightly. Scald milk and melt margarine together. Poor over sugar and salt. Add beaten eggs and yeast mixture. Stir in approximately 9 - 10 cups of flour. Keep dough quite sticky. Let rise till double.

Roll dough out to about 1/2-inch thick, rectangle shape. Spread with 3/4 cup melted margarine, a layer of brown sugar and sprinkle with cinnamon. Roll up from long side. Slice in 1-inch thick slices. Place in greased round pie or cake tins, leaving 1/4 inch between rolls. Let rise till double. Bake at 325 degrees for 20 - 25 minutes. Turn rolls out of pans on to paper plate and right side up to cool. Makes approximately eight nine-inch round tins.

Butter Cream Icing

1 cup shortening	8 cups powdered sugar
1 cup margarine	4 tablespoons milk
2 teaspoons vanilla	

Cream shortening and margarine. Add milk and vanilla, mix together and beat in powdered sugar on medium until light and fluffy, three to five minutes. Frost rolls when cool.

A friend loves at all times.
~ Proverbs 17:17 ~

Cousin's Portraits

❧

If a task is once begun, never leave it til it's done.
Be the labor great or small, do it well or not at all.

Four-month-old Sierra was coming for a visit with her parents. We hadn't seen her for over a month and we could hardly wait for her to arrive. It was 10:30 pm when the family stumbled in, wearied from their eight-hour journey.

Aunt Carla, Grandpa and I were alert and ready. We quickly grabbed the little car seat full of baby and lightly pulled the blanket from her sleeping body. Slowly, her eyes opened with little blinks and she began to smile at the strange faces huddled so close to her tiny cheeks. What a princess she was. She yawned and cooed and wondered at the commotion and this strange place. At last, Grandma carried the little one to her awaiting crib; however, Sierra was not at all comfortable with these new surroundings and she began to wail. Nothing settled the sweet blessing. For a half-hour she screamed and then finally she took her pacifier and fell asleep.

At 8:00 the next morning she was up and smiling. Grandma toted her about and Aunt Carla changed her from pajamas to new outfits in just a few minutes. She carried her off to show everyone in the house and then changed her back into her pajamas. The tiny one smiled, then puckered, then started that process over again.

Sierra and her cousin Kyle, who lived close by us, were going to have pictures with Aunt Carla during that particular visit. For a month now, Carla had been seeking out the perfect outfits. After purchasing and returning different ones, Carla had settled on a small red tee shirt with denim shorts for 9-month-old Kyle and a red striped tee shirt with a tiny denim skirt for Sierra. We wondered and worried over getting the babies to sleep at the correct moment, making the appointment for the photos exactly at the time both babies woke up and then getting the perfect smiles on the two little ones at the exact perfect second.

The day quickly arrived to accomplish this feat. Kyle woke up hot with a fever of 104 degrees so we sponged him and called the doctor.

We nursed and cuddled the little guy hour after hour. Photos were forgotten.

The next day arrived much the same way. The tots preferred nothing more than kind, gentle attention. There was no chance of jostling them off to a photographer.

On day three of the visit, we gave up the idea of dragging babies out and sat up a studio in our living room. As Sierra lay on her tummy, Kyle crawled over her. Next, he crawled toward our flapping, waving arms. We were making such a racket to attract the babies eyes to the right place and get some sort of smile, that instead we brought fright and tears. Two unbecoming snaps and the whole process was scrapped.

On the fourth and final day of Sierra's visit, we still had no pictures with Auntie. We raced home from church Sunday evening with one goal in mind. Each baby ate their bedtime feedings and clothes were rapidly changed. Everyone moved swiftly to the basement and Bob flipped on the gas fireplace, which would serve as the background. Quickly, before any fusses, the babies were positioned with Aunt Carla. The other five folk made every kind of clicking and rattling noise possible. We tried to distract Kyle from mauling Sierra's face and keep their attention focused toward the camera then with one click after another we snapped the pictures.

Everyone was exhausted from the effort we had each exerted to make this happen. We were stumbling over each other all giggling at how the other person preformed, and loudly praising our babies for how well they had done. There weren't many smiles, but we had gotten some pleasant expressions anyway. We celebrated the whole undertaking with ice cream, cake, chips and dips. These babies were our daughters' first children, Bob's and my first grandbabies, Carla's first nephew and niece and the babies' first cousins. Oh, we were enjoying snapping photos to keep for first memories; memories that will remain for a lifetime. ✄

Section Four

Grandma's Heart

...the unfeigned faith...
which dwelt first in thy grandmother Lois...
and I am persuaded that in thee also.
~ 2 Timothy 1:5 KJV ~

Grandmother's Wisdom

*I long to put the experience
of fifty years at once into
your young lives,
to give you at once
the key of that treasure chamber
every gem of which has cost me tears
and struggles and prayer,
but you must work for these inward
treasures yourself.*

~ Harrriet Beecher Stow ~

Tea Time with Daddy

I really do believe it:
The beauty I see over tea is thee.
~ Emily Barnes ~

My son-in-law, Rod, had a day off from work. Twenty-two-month old Kyle was exuberant. It was hard for him to leave his daddy's side for his much needed afternoon nap; however, his mother knew that the rest would make an important difference during the remainder of his afternoon.

After waking from his nap, Kyle went to the kitchen for his snack. "Nack... nack," he said. Suddenly he remembered that daddy was outside working. He exclaimed to his mommy with a look that said, "I just remembered!" and said, "Daddy, nack?" Christa replied, "Oh, do you want to have a snack with Daddy?"

With that, Kyle proceeded to collect two muffins and carried them to his little table by the window, all the while declaring "daddy ... nack, daddy ... nack." The young man marched back to the kitchen continuing his little chant and interrupted that with, "Mommy, juice ... juice ... Daddy ... Kyle?" Away he went with juice in hand to the awaiting table still exclaiming, "Daddy ... nack, Daddy ... nack." Setting the cups in the right spot, he noticed one chair was missing. Glancing around the house, Kyle spied the absent chair in another room. He pushed and shoved until it was positioned just right, endlessly repeating, "Daddy ... nack, Daddy ... nack, Daddy ... nack." It now appeared to this excited chap that his tea party was now ready. He went to the door and called out, "Daddyyy ... naaack!"

As usual, Daddy responded to his young son and came in to find this delightful party all in place; each piece carefully put together with love by his son. Father and son sat down to enjoy a first of hopefully many blissful snack times together. The conversation centered on a few words. "Daddy, working, tools, house, juice, Kyle, baby, Mommy." Christa stood quietly out of the way as she beamed her happiness over her son and his father, both appearing as enthused as the other with this party for two.

That evening when Christa detailed this entire story to me, my thoughts went to the incredible delight of little Kyle waiting for his daddy to join him. As I mused over this pleasurable exchange between father and son, I recalled the joy I had when I collected my hot cup of tea, Bible and journal and sat down with my heavenly Father on a day I needed a fresh reminder of His love. The Lord responded promptly to me as I called on Him, just as Kyle's daddy laid down his tools and came to his child when he called, "Daddyyy ... naaack!"

As a father has compassion on his children, so the Lord has compassion on those who fear him;
~ Psalm 103:13 ~

Dedicated to the Lord

Three-month-old Sierra had learned so many things since the day she was born. Along with sleeping through the long nights, she had also found her toys. She intently watched them as she smiled and talked. At times she'd burst into a little giggle—especially when Aunt Carla played with her. One quiet evening when both grandmas were visiting, Sierra's mommy had her doing the sweetest laughter. We grandmothers were sitting on the edge of our chairs completely enjoying every tiny noise.

The next day was Sunday and a special day for Sierra and her parents. She looked like a little princess in her freshly starched white frock. Her bright blue eyes and dark hair were shining, giving her a heavenly glow. It was the day Sierra's parents had chosen to have a public dedication for their baby, giving her back to their heavenly Father. We gathered around Sierra in the front of the church and several people laid hands on her tiny head as the pastor and Grandpa led the congregation of Christian friends in heartfelt prayers of dedication. Sierra was an angel. She smiled as the pastor compassionately conferred with the Lord on her behalf. Her Uncle Jon sang a verse of a song that touched our hearts:

> *How sweet to hold a newborn baby,*
> *And feel the pride, and joy he gives;*
> *But greater still the calm assurance,*
> *This child can face uncertain days because He lives.*

Quietly she lay and listened in her mother's arms. Sierra, our miracle baby girl:

> *Because He lives I can face tomorrow,*
> *Because He lives all fear is gone;*
> *Because I know He holds the future.*
> *And life is worth the living just because He lives.*

The Open Staircase

All that I am or ever hope to be,
I owe to my angel Mother.
~ Abraham Lincoln ~

Christa sat baby Kyle on the living room floor and took off his jacket. She went to the kitchen to get herself a drink of water. The little guy spied the open staircase and felt his freedom. As quickly as his newly learned crawl could take him, he pattered to the steps.

Two minutes later, his mother returned to the living room. To her shock, Kyle was only three steps from the top of that staircase. Quickly and quietly, she glided up behind him as not to cause him alarm and stood sheltered behind her tiny 7-month-old boy.

This little scene painted a vivid picture in my mind of what the following verse really looks like:

The angel of the Lord encamps around those who fear Him.
~ Psalm 34:7 ~

Kyle's New Bedroom

*To love what you do and feel that it matters —
how could anything be more fun?*

Ten-month-old Kyle was getting a new bedroom and excitement mounted for mommy and Aunt Carla. Searching for the perfect wall paper took hours, then came the curtains and wall decor. Kyle couldn't conceive this enthusiasm since he was much to young to understand that in a few short weeks his baby sibling would arrive.

Daddy neatly pasted the chosen paper to the walls. Giraffes and bunnies dotted the room and looked completely pleasant for Kyle's rambunctious personality. A new chest of drawers with shelves lined with books and stuffed animals stood against one wall. The rocking chair was moved in and a toy horse sat under the window.

A new oak crib was purchased and while Grandpa and Daddy were busy in the yard, Grandma took the electric screwdriver in hand and put it together. Pushing it against the right wall, Mommy, Carla and Grandma covered the mattress with fresh sheets and a bumper pad. Noah's ark animals splashed across the bed leaving a quiet, finished feeling to the whole room.

Kyle found this new adventure so exciting that he immediately wanted in the new crib. We picked+ him up and did just that in an effort to make his new surroundings feel secure. He buzzed from one end of the bed to the other with squeals of delight.

For the first few days when Kyle was tucked in for naps and night times with prayers and hugs, sad little cries burst out. It took him about a week to adjust, but he was peacefully contented with his new surroundings before his tiny baby sister, Kassondra Brooke, arrived just two days after he turned one. 🦜

To everything there is a season, and a time to every purpose under heaven.
~ Ecclesiastes 3:1 KJV ~

Our First Visit to Sierra

*I begin to love this little creature, and to anticipate her birth
as a fresh twist to a knot which I do not wish to untie.*
~ Mary Wallstonecraft ~

We had traveled to our daughter's home on many occasions
and each time we wandered in tired and spent from the eight- hour
journey. We always greeted one another cheerfully and then I would
scan the meticulous perfection of her warm home, with not one item out
of place.

Later, when Sierra was three months old, her Aunt Carla,
Grandpa and I, once again traveled the ever familiar pathway. We
stumbled into the house in our usual worn manner and hugged Rachel,
now a mother. Then we saw tiny Sierra lying on the floor. Oh, the joy!
For so many years we waited, prayed and longed for a tiny one to live in
this family.

As we three stood over Sierra that evening she gave us her
biggest and brightest smiles. She blew bubbles and talked with her lips
pursed together in a most delightful manner. We held her and boasted
over her bulging checks and the irresistible double chin that was just
like Great Grandma's.

Some time later, when I was able to think of other things, I
glanced around the once perfectly ordered house. What a lovely treasure
met my eyes. Scattered here and there were baby blankets, little pink
sleepers, a bouncer seat and extra toys. A swing sat in one corner with a
cradle in another. Nursing needs lay at one end of the table and a freshly
folded diaper at the other. How refreshing to observe the untidiness of
this once precisely kept home. One of life's richest blessings had been
placed here; a tiny baby girl.

Never in all of the years that we live and breath can we express
the gratitude deep in our hearts for this cherished miracle, little Sierra
Janae, which means "God replied."

For this child we prayed.
~ l Samuel 1:27 KJV ~

Encouraging Pastor Grandpa

The art of being wise is the art of knowing what to overlook.
~ *William James* ~

At age 1, Kyle loved to spot Grandpa at the front of the church preaching the Word. Each Sunday he would put his arm straight out and point up to Grandpa, hollering out his endearing word for him, "Daaaaa," as the biggest and brightest smile spread across his face. After several moments of this, Pastor Grandpa would find it difficult to keep his poised manner and at last responded back with a delightful beam that connected with his grandson. Encouraged by the admiration of this little man, with new fervor Grandpa continued the message.

As the same scenario happened again one morning, I thought of several times when the Lord focused directly upon me and enthusiastically ministered great encouragement to my heart, exactly when I needed it. Recently, within a group of friends, I had sensed some tension, which made me want to retreat and quietly move to the background. At that moment, the Lord called my name, "Donna." He freed me from the bondage of fear by His very presence and acceptance. His admiration and abiding love for me is even deeper than that of Kyle's delight in his grandfather.

There have been many times when I've been the one to call out to my Father and feel Him respond to me in a beam of warmth, love and empowerment for my immediate situation. No matter what my lot at any given moment, the enjoyment of my Lord and His Presence with me gives encouragement like no other. 🌿

The Lord is my light and my salvation; whom shall I fear?
The Lord is the strength of my life; of whom shall I be afraid?
~ Psalm 27:1 AV ~

An Easter Sunday

A grandchild is a precious gift, and so is a grandmother's love.

I filled the pretty wire basket with many kinds of tempting Easter treats, then stuck it away until naps were finished.

My niece Shari, her husband Nick and their 18-month-old daughter Natalie, had come for a weekend visit. Christa and her family joined us for lunch, then we tucked the three babies, all who were under two, in for afternoon rests.

I could hardly wait until they got up. My treat was ready and I was eager to explain the Easter story to my grandbabies and great niece for the very first time. As they were still staggering from their sleep, I pulled out the basket. All three huddled around me on the living room floor and six little hands eagerly reached into the basket before I even had time to think.

As the tots stuffed jellybeans and marshmallow bunnies into their mouths, I became aware that I needed to talk fast about the first Easter ever. "And so Jesus died many years ago," I was declaring as Kyle wanted Natalie's chocolate egg. "Christa, get them each their own bowl," I said in the same sentence as, "Today is the day we celebrate that Jesus came back to life."

I paused here briefly to help 10-month-old Kassondra get another marshmallow chick, "And when you each get older ... " I continued as Shari snapped pictures and I was interrupted again to move Natalie's dish from Kyle's long arm. Christa was saying, "Mom, I think that's enough candy." Carla went running for wash clothes and I continued, "You'll hear Jesus knocking at your heart," and I quickly stammered through, "and He'll forgive all your sins!" Whew, the story was finished.

Chocolate, marshmallow and jellybean juices were dripping everywhere. The daddy's weren't sure the babies had heard any of the story, let alone understood it. However, to this new grandma, who is all about teaching and making memories, this was a first at describing the blessed story of old that grants us our cleansing and promises us eternity with Jesus.

At Easter time for over a decade, my own daughters listened to this master story from their mother and father. We would not alter this magnificent, important tradition now or in the days to come. As messy as it all was, everyone delighted in the rapid five-minute experience. And were we glad to wash up the babies and hide the basket from their ever-quick hands. ✐

He arose! He arose!
Hallelujah! Christ arose!

He is not here; but is risen!
~ Luke 24:6 ~

Tell me the Stories of Jesus

William H. Parker, 1904

First let me hear how the children stood round His knee,
And I shall fancy His blessing resting on me;
Words full of kindness, deeds full of grace,
All in the love light of Jesus' face.

(Chorus)
Tell me the stories of Jesus I love to hear;
Things I would ask Him to tell me
If He were here; Scenes by the wayside,
Tales of the sea, Stories of Jesus,
Tell them to me.

Tell me, in accents of wonder, how rolled the sea,
Tossing the boat in a tempest on Galilee;
And how the Maker, ready and kind,
Chided the billows, and hushed the wind.

Into the city I'd follow the children's band,
Waving a branch of the palm tree high in my hand.
One of His heralds, yes, I would sing
Loudest hosannas, & Jesus is King!

Show me that scene in the garden, of bitter pain.
Show me the cross where my Savior for me was slain.
Sad ones or bright ones, so that they be
Stories of Jesus, tell them to me.

Jessica

A good laugh is sunshine in a house.

Jessica was coming for the morning and we were busily preparing for her arrival. Jessica, a 6 year old special-needs child, has Retts Syndrome and isn't able to walk or talk like most children do. Still, she loves excitement and life. Right on time, Jessica's mother came bounding in the door with her silent, beaming girl in tow.

It happened on that particular day that 9-month-old Kyle was also at our home. He hadn't seen Jessica for quite some time and was delighted to have her for his playmate. Kyle would do his natural antics, which marvelously amused Jessica. She sat on the floor across from him and chuckled to her joyful hearts content. Kyle wasn't at all disturbed that Jessica's play was different from his. He was pleasantly excited to share all he could with her, and to receive bountifully from her extraordinary gifts.

The light in the eyes [of him whose heart is joyful]
rejoices the hearts of others.
~ Proverbs 15:30 AMP ~

Baby's Blanket

Character building begins in our infancy and continues until death.
~ Eleanor Roosevelt ~

While visiting Rachel's home, I put 3-month-old Sierra in her crib. I wrapped the pastel green comforter tightly around her body and laid her soft pink blanket on the comforter about eight inches back from her little round face.

Minutes later, I peeked in to see if my grandbaby had gone to sleep and I couldn't believe what I saw. Sierra had pulled the pink blanket up and it was laying across a portion of her sleeping face. I could not imagine how Sierra's short little arms and tiny hands could accomplish this task. I went to Rachel and explained to her what Sierra had done. "Oh," Rachel said, "She does that, it's so interesting to watch her."

Somehow this tiny baby was able to reach around until she found the fuzzy blanket and with her miniature fingers she tugged and pulled until it snuggled against her cheek. This was such a lesson to me of the power of the Lord in my life. I can accomplish the tasks that look impossible if I work at them with all my strength, exactly as my newborn grandbaby was able to do. She found just what she wanted and placed it exactly where she wanted it. 🦋

Whatsoever thy hand findeth to do, do it with all thy might;
~ Ecclesiastes 9:10 KJV ~

Backyard Camping

All of life is a gift, and
God has given it for joy.
~ Terry Lindvall ~

In the time span of one year, we were blessed with our first three grandchildren. With all the tiny ones around, the idea of a family camping weekend that summer was scraped. "It would be much too hard," my daughters declared. "Okay," I decided, "We'll camp at home!"

Rachel, Glen and 8-month-old Sierra arrived for a long weekend. Carla, Rachel and Christa decided to leave the three babies in my care and head for the city. I was delighted and the four of us set out to create family memories. We would build a campsite in the back yard.

Dragging armloads of babies, chairs, roasting sticks, toys, a tent and grill out the door and down the steps in a dozen trips, I just couldn't contain the little bursts of giggles and excitement I felt. I was making camping memories for the very first time with my three grandbabies.

Kyle, the oldest, had just turned 1 and had been walking for all of two days. He was in the height of his glory toddling all around this campsite. He'd pull the tent poles out as soon as I'd push one in. I'd exclaim, "Kyle, isn't this the grandest of fun? We're going to make camping happen right here in the backyard." I would sing, "Camping memories with the babies," and we'd all laugh with glee.

Sierra sat cheerfully on her blanket with toys all around her playing pat-a-cake and observing every part of this camping expedition. Kyle's 2-week-old sister, Kassondra, was fast asleep in her little basket. It was perched on the patio table that had also been lugged to the campsite. She was enjoying the whole process almost as much as her grandma.

I'd shove the next set of tent poles in and over on the other side, Kyle would pull another set out. Oh, we chuckled. Well, if I imagined correctly, we chuckled. However, without the imagination I was the only one doing the chuckling. The other three were simply doing their first-year-of-life kind of activities. I exclaimed to the babies how this tent is getting old and torn up. We conversed all about their mommies and Aunt Carla sleeping in it when they were little girls. "Soon Grandpa will need to purchase another," I announced. The three quietly appeared to enjoy the non-stop chatter of their grandmother, or at least they continued contentedly with their activities.

Late in the afternoon Carla, Rachel and Christa arrived home from the shopping spree and wandered to the back yard. They kidded about Grandma making memories with three babies under one. "Memories for Grandma or who?" they wondered aloud. The tent still needed set up since I had finally decided to put the tent stakes out of Kyle's reach and wait for help. All four of us were either singing, babbling or sleeping with satisfied pleasure.

Rachel grabbed hold of the other side of the tent and the two of us got it raised. Christa sat down to feed baby Kassie and Carla snuggled with Sierra as she showed her the purchases the three had brought home with them.

"It's the grandest way to camp," I expressed to my unenthused daughters, "We can sleep in our own beds, fix food in our own kitchen and wash dishes at our own sink. The babies are loving every minute of it," I proclaimed. You would never have known we weren't "really" camping as we grilled chicken and sat up a picnic table right there on site, except for the luxury of running to the house for all the things we'd forgotten.

The men arrived on the scene and wondered at the sight. They clucked out comments to their mother-in-law and her ingenious ideas. Just then, the tent that was awaiting the strong arms of a male to hammer in the stakes, burst up with a gush of wind and began floating away from the secured camping spot, much to the delight of my sons-in-law. Deep inside they loved the at-home camping as much as I did. They golfed in the back yard and wandered through weeds searching for balls. They played catch and roasted marshmallows with pleasure.

After enjoying Kyle and Sierra's excitable play for an hour in the tent, everyone determined Grandma's dreamy idea of camping in the back yard with tent included wasn't such a bad idea after all. Well after dark, Rod, Christa and babies headed for the comforts of their home a few miles away, as the rest of us wandered into our comfy, cozy beds. ✻

Be content with what you have.
~ Hebrews 13:5 ~

Face to Face

Longing for God creates an intensity of spirit.
~ Joel Gregory ~

Christa laid tiny 3-week-old Kassondra on Aunt Carla's bed. One could never predict what her 12-month-old brother might do to his baby sister, so Christa pulled the door shut behind her. The three of us women continued about our work.

A little while later, Carla went into her bedroom, shut the door, checked the baby, grabbed something she needed and came back out, closing the door tightly once again.

After a spell, I wondered outloud, "Where is Kyle?" The quietness called for a search that turned up nothing, so I suggested checking Carla's bedroom. "Well, how could he be in there?" the girls wondered. Carla decided to make a quick scan to satisfy her mother.

There on the bed, lying face to face, were baby brother and sister, each gazing into the other's eyes. Big brother wasn't doing any unkindness to baby, but his rustling had awakened her. It was the sweetest scene – face to face, tiny sister and brother.

We concluded that when Carla came back out of her bedroom after checking the baby, the little man darted in unknown to her. I felt a stir in my heart to experience face to face fellowship with the Lord at any cost. Kyle was always eager to be close to his sister and found a way to make that happen no matter what the obstacle. ✺

Face to face with Christ my Saviour,
Face to face – what will it be,
When with rapture I behold Him,
Jesus Christ, who died for me?

All Better

Who ran to help me when I fell,
And would some pretty story tell,
Or kiss the place to make it well?
My mother.
~ Ann Taylor ~

Sierra was intrigued by the stone slab that lay in front of our fireplace. She stumbled up that one-inch step and then toppled down it, repeating this activity over and over. I was thrilled in my heart as I watched the little girl, now 14 months old, as she merrily enjoyed her second Christmas, this time at Grandpa's house.

Suddenly, she made a squeal. I turned to her as she caught herself from a fall off the hearth stone. Sensing something was wrong, I quickly went to her. She picked up her two small hands, which were blistering rapidly. She had fallen onto the burning hot glass that secured the blazing fire behind it. There on the fireproof glass were her tiny handprints.

We quickly ran cold water over her hands as Grandpa raced away to his office to get some burn spray he had there. Sierra's Uncle Rod suggested, "Toothpaste is supposed to help the pain." We tried everything we knew but to little avail. I felt heart sick that the pleasantries of Sierra's second Christmas were spoiled and I chided myself for not thinking of a screen for the front of the hot glass. We wrapped her chubby little hands, sealing in the ointment, and cuddled, soothed and rocked the little one for the rest of the day.

Day after day Rachel lovingly redressed Sierra's hands. We prayed over them and encouraged her through the moments she felt most distressed. The big blisters got tender, larger, redder and sorer. One day, her parents discovered that slowly, the fingertips were beginning to heal. Then the blisters on each hand started shrinking, becoming shriveled and wrinkled. Each day mommy watched for infection and felt encouraged as the hands continued to show growth of new pink skin.

At long last, several weeks after the accident as Rachel checked

Sierra's hands once again, she said, "All better, no need for bandages today." The two of them studied and looked at her tiny hands together. Cheerfully Sierra ran off, free of the cumbersome wrappings. The next morning Mommy looked at her hands again and exclaimed, "All better." Sierra echoed her response in her tiny voice. The next morning and the next, Sierra continued to rejoice with those little words to her daddy and then to her mommy as she sung "All better."

As my daughter relayed these story parts to me, I remembered the recent dark tunnel the Lord allowed me to go through. It held intense pain and trial that stretched into weeks, just as the hurt in Sierra's hands did. I felt that my prayers for a day of calm seemed without hope. Tiny Sierra appeared to wonder if her hands would ever grip her toys again without pain. Would she ever not hurt when she stumbled and caught herself with her tender fingers? Would the touch of the warm bath water ever again feel pleasant, rather than painful?

The scriptures promise me light at the end of my darkness. In my process, the Lord hovered around me and bandaged my wounds, even as Sierra's mama did hers. He carefully watched over my pain, and then, as light began to dawn in my heart, the Lord rejoiced with me as He watched new growth and deeper faith forming in me. When my mourning turned to joy, I rejoiced and felt all better, just as Sierra did.

For I will turn their mourning into joy, and comfort them,
and make them rejoice from their sorrow.
~ Jeremiah 31:13 KJV ~

Overjoyed Kassondra

Twenty-two-month-old Kyle was ill with a fever. Hour after hour his mother sat rocking the little guy, wearied from three nights of little sleep. I stopped in about noon the third day of this rendezvous. The tiny family looked just as it felt outside; downcast, dreary and ready to burst drops of warm, rainy tears.

As baby Kassondra spied me, she wiggled, giggled and squealed her delight. I picked up Kassie as Christa lazily said, "Pardon the matted hair. She was sitting cheerfully in her highchair while I rocked Kyle, so I left her there." The baby had enjoyed not only feeding herself, but also squishing and smearing her food so much that she smelled like a bowl of spaghetti. Her usual strawberry-blond hair showed nearly an orange-red tint from the gooey sauce slathered through it. Elated with some attention, 10-month-old Kassie hugged her grandma with glee.

I took my turn rocking Kyle while mommy savored a few minutes with Kassie and tidied a neglected house. I prayed over the feverish little man and we talked stories of Grandpa, Daddy and tools. Then I left for home with the enraptured, squiggly Kassondra in tow.

My mind went to the kindness of the Lord's love ministering even to the tiniest during a desolate time. Baby Kassie couldn't have displayed her joy over her needs being met in a more exuberant way. This sweet scene reminded me of the delight I felt when feeling rejected some time ago, I opened my Bible and read Psalm 103:4. I envisioned the Lord lovingly piecing together a crown with beautiful spring flowers and then compassionately placing it on my head for me to rest in His acceptance of me. It gave me the warmest sense of value just as my little granddaughter felt on her rather lonely day.

He took the children in his arms, put his hands on them and blessed them.
Mark 10:16

Staying In His Shadow

Sometimes relinquishment means giving up a cherished dream, a plan, an illusion. Life is often a series of adjustments — fitting our dreams to reality.
~ Ruth Sentra ~

Six-month-old Sierra was sitting in the bright sunshine on the living room floor and all around her tiny form lay her gray shadow. Sierra stretched out her hand to pick up that dark shape for play. When it didn't join her clasped hand, she grabbed at the form, but it continued to lie still, which began to frustrate her. Taking her stubby fingers, she clawed the carpet in a frantic effort of getting that presence into her hands. Her desperate unmet desires gave way to wails of discouragement.

This little story reminded me of the promises in Psalm 91:1, "He who dwells in the secret place of the most High, shall abide under the shadow of the Almighty." As long as Sierra stayed sitting in that same spot on the carpeted floor, her shadow hovered around her and she could not move it. No matter what sort of effort she put forth, she could not get away from the shadow.

I felt falsely accused one day and knew my self-pity was standing in the way of enjoying the Lord's presence. David says in Psalm 91, "if I linger or rest in the secret place of the Lord, His shadow will never leave my side." Nothing I do can remove the Lord's presence from me, if I, as Sierra did, remain settled there. I had to confess my sinful selfishness that day and get back under the shadow of His presence. My frayed feelings changed to the peace that comes from dwelling in His secret place.

He who dwells in the shelter of the Most High will rest in the shadow of the Almighty.
~ Psalm 91:1 ~

Section Six

Extended
Family
Treasures

The lines are fallen unto me in pleasant places;
yea I have a goodly heritage.
~ Psalm 16:6 KJV ~

Paddleboat Escapade

The child you want to raise as an upright and honorable person requires a lot more of your time than your money.
~ George Varky ~

When 8-year-old Christa learned there were inflatable paddleboats on the market, it was very tempting for her to own one. Her friend Anthony had one and she thought it looked like fun. Just down over the hill lay peaceful Beaver Lake, a body of water that was surrounded by trees, keeping it quiet and calm, just perfect for canoeing or paddleboating.

The longer Christa pondered this paddleboat idea, the more she desired to purchase one. Upon discussing the notion with her father, the two settled on a goal, leaving Christa to come up with a plan to earn the few needed dollars. With this purpose in mind it was not hard for her to aquire the money and soon she was on her way to the Canadian Tire store where the boat was chosen and tucked under her arm. As she gave the clerk her hard-earned dollars, a bright smile formed across her face and we marched to the car with her new purchase.

A few days later, Christa's cousins from Wisconsin arrived for a summer time visit and gave the new paddleboat a great workout. With life jackets snapped securely in place, these young ones pushed from shore again and again that week. They paddled quietly around Beaver Lake for hours, listening to loons call and watching for jumping fish. They peered at birds flying overhead and observed a school of young fish swim past.

I considered the energy my motivated daughter exerted to earn the money for this important purchase. Along with that, I pondered over her excitement of filling that boat with air and pushing from shore for the very first time. It led me to believe there were life lessons of responsibility and stewardship in this whole experience for Christa.

I will instruct you and teach you in the way you should go;
I will counsel you and watch over you.
~ Psalm 32:8 ~

Gifts of Love

Somehow not only for Christmas
but all the long year through,
The joy that you give other's
is the joy that comes back to you.
~ John Greenleaf Whittier ~

It was Christmas 1985 — a day set aside to celebrate the greatest love gift ever given. One by one, cousins, aunts and uncles spilled into Grandma's cozy, sprawling farmhouse. The dairy farm held precious memories, as well as promises of another fun-filled day for this growing family.

The food, cookies and candy treats that ladened the tables were quickly eaten amongst the delightful chatter. The hours of play time and topic debates kept moments rolling all too rapidly.

At long last, the children believed it was time to share our gifts of love. One by one, eager grandchildren were handed their brightly wrapped packages. The seven little girls began tearing open identical looking gifts. Pleasant smiles spread across their faces as each took furry flannel nightgowns from their

wrappings. Every garment had been stitched together with love by their grandmother. And that wasn't all, for folded neatly with each larger gown was a tiny one for each of the younger granddaughter's doll baby.

Late that evening, a parade of young girls decked out in fuzzy long gowns with dollies matching came into the family room. Aunts immediately began positioning little girls in some sort of order to get pictures of these children outfitted in their gifts of love. Cameras were ready to snap just as seven-year-old Christa's foot caught under Grandma's rocking chair. Grandma, sharing yet another love gift, comforted Christa as warmly as those snug gowns felt, and dried her tears. Quickly, before anything else could happen, cameras clicked and flashed.

As I watched these little girls treasure their gifts of love from Grandma, I had to consider my response to my heavenly Father about the greatest gift ever given. I want my joy for the price of my salvation to far exceed these little girls' excitement over their home-sewn nightgowns from Grandma. 🍃

And she shall bring forth a son, and thou shalt call his name JESUS:
~ Matthew 1:21 ~

The Sinking Canoe

Those who bring sunshine to the lives
of others cannot keep it from themselves
~ James M. Barrie ~

The girls' cousin Amy accompanied her grandparents for a visit to our northern home one summer. Rachel and Amy, both 12 years old, reminded me so much of twins as I looked in on their activity during those fun-packed days.

One particularly warm afternoon, the girls decided upon a canoe party. Grandma was concerned the water would be too cold for Amy per chance the canoe tipped. Reluctantly, but obediently, Amy did as her grandma instructed and sat among the rocks sticking first her toes, then her feet into the water. She was to do this slowly so her body could adjust to the cooler northern water temperature. Once the water level reached above her knees, Grandma was satisfied.

The girls stuffed themselves into orange life jackets, hopped aboard the canoe and shoved into the lake. Carla and her friend Mary grabbed a second canoe and joined the other pair.

Girl talk and contagious laughter hyped the enthusiasm of these four. Purposely, Carla and Mary flipped their canoe; took a quick dip and pulled themselves back inside, thus inspiring the younger, less experienced girls to try the same thing. Slowly Rachel and Amy moved to one side of the canoe and suddenly, before they were ready, they were in the water.

After the shocking dip in the lake, with their heads bobbing above the bright life jackets, the girls' four flailing arms grabbing for the canoe only caused reason for more thrills. Each latched onto the same end of the watercraft and tried to hoist themselves back inside. Their weight pulled it down and buckets of water spilled in causing a much greater dilemma. These two adolescents then decided on tipping the canoe in an effort to empty it, only to watch even more water pour in.

After some time with no success, they humbly called to the older two friends for help. Carla and Mary went to the aid of the stranded and some hours later, this bunch of girls lugged that water-logged canoe to the shore. Each were still chuckling as they puttered up the rocky hill and fell exhausted into chairs to rest.

This treasured memory from that week-long visit tells a tale of how hard I was working to get myself out of a guilt-plagued mind a one day. Worn out, I finally called to the Lord for help. He walked with me and lightened my load. Certainly that was the feeling of Amy and Rachel as Carla and Mary tugged along side of them, helping to bear their very heavy burden. Grandma was ever so delightfully happy to have those girls safely back on dry land. 🔗

And my God will meet all your needs according to
His glorious riches in Christ Jesus.
~ Philippians 4:19 ~

Our Father's World

*A happy home and family is the
source of the greatest human happiness.*

We pulled on bulky life jackets one peaceful summer afternoon and wandered down the hill to the crystal clear lake. Carla, 12, Rachel, 11, and Christa, 8, were excited to have their cousin Joe visiting for the summer months. Joe, 16, enjoyed nothing more than afternoons in our rustic boat, paddling quietly around the lake. Many times he would throw out his fishing line and once in awhile he actually got a bite.

We'd nibble on a picnic lunch or nestle down with a good book as we slowly drifted and bobbed this way and that. The blue sky reflected perfectly in the tranquil water around us. A loon would call periodically and flap across, leaving ripples along its path. Nearby, a fish would jump two feet out of the water and dive immediately back in.

We visited softly about the bliss of nature and the creation days when the Lord meticulously formed each part of this earth by His spoken word. We marveled at the stillness and quietly hummed:

*This is my Father's world,
The birds their carols raise,
The morning bright, the lily white,
Declare their Maker's praise.*

God saw all that He had made, and it was very good.
~ Genesis 1:31 ~

A Summer to Remember

Christa's cousin Nathan, two years younger than herself, moved with his parents to the old family farmhouse, just down the road. These two were excited to have each other close-by and made plans to do every creative kind of fun they could that summer.

Each had received brand new bikes, which added to these intentions. Nathan had even gotten a speedometer for his. The pair raced on their bikes for miles while Nathan clocked exactly how far they went and just how fast. Up and down the road they would go. First, Christa was ahead, but when she wore out and her pace slowed, Nathan was the leader; back and forth the contests went.

Exactly halfway between the two homes there was a small creek where Nathan and Christa would meet after making plans over the phone. Carefully, the two crawled under the bridge and would spend many an hour in the little creek. They built dams with rocks to stop the water from its natural flow and then they'd watch as it swirled around the rocks, desperate to continue on its way. Little schools of fish sped rapidly by, much to fast for these quick hands and nets to snatch them. There were worms and butterflies that became the possession of this team; little nests in plastic cups kept the worms secure and jars with holes in the lids worked perfect for the butterflies.

Christa was to attend the same school as Nathan in the fall, so he did his part to ensure she knew the ropes of all the sports activities she would need to be involved in. They played volleyball over the clothes line and shot baskets in the hoop in the driveway. Bats, balls and mits were collected and entertained hard workouts week after week.

Those were precious memory-making hours and special times of bonding for cousins. It happened there was only one summer when these two lived just down the road from each other, but that one summer was packed full of most delightful treasures.

Be very careful how you live — making
the most of every opportunity.
~ Ephesians 5:15 ~

Creative Cousins

*Precious memories, warm moments with those we love and
wishes for many more to come.*

Grandpa and Grandma drove the many miles to our home in
northern Ontario quite regularly. Accompanying them on one particular
journey was Randy, who was Carla, Rachel and Christa's fun-loving
cousin. These four young children had a grand week exploring and
creating together.

It was early one morning when I glanced out the window and
saw Randy, 4, and Rachel, 3, wandering back from a stroll. Still donned
in pajama's, with the sun barely cresting the horizon, this pair had been
on a nature hike. There is something about rising early and going out
into nature. Even our Lord gave us this example when He rose a great
while before day and went out to pray.

These young cousins knew the bliss of opening their new day in
the presence of nature; the rising of the sun, the early morning chirping
of the birds and the quiet, calm of the lake down the hill.

*And in the morning, rising a great while before day, he went out, and
departed into a solitary place, and there prayed.*
~ Mark 1:35 KJV ~

Merry Sleigh Ride

*December gifts — custom, ceremony, celebration, consecration — come to us
wrapped up, not in tissue and ribbons, but in cherished memories.*
~ Sarah Ban Breathnach ~
(Simple Abundancy)

It was Christmas 1974 and the blustery cold in Michigan yielded plenty of snow. This magnificent weather called for a sleigh ride, so my father hitched the horse team to the wagon on skies.

Bundling the household of grandchildren as warm as possible andcollecting warm blankets, we moms hauled everyone to the awaiting sleigh. Carla was 20 months old and the first one lifted on to the large sled. Perched way up high on a bale of straw, packaged in her very warm coat, scarf and mitts, she looked like a snow queen.

"All aboard," my dad called when the sleigh was loaded with passengers and with a quick jerk we were off. There were nine siblings, several who were married and seven grandchildren. The whole bunch of of us rode with delightful chatter and gales of laughter along down the road.

These were fun and important times together as a family. The experience of this first sleigh ride for tiny Carla was the beginning link in the chain of many more happy extended family treasures. ✌

The children of your people will live in security.
~ Psalm 102:28 NLT ~

Precious Memories

J.B.F. Wright, b. 1877

Precious mem'ries, unseen angels,
Sent from somewhere to my soul;
How they linger, ever near me,
And the sacred past unfold.

(Chorus)
Precious mem'ries, How they linger,
How they ever flood my soul,
In the stillness of the midnight,
Precious, sacred scenes unfold.

Precious father, loving mother,
Fly across the lonely years,
And old home scenes of my child-hood,
In fond memory appears.

In the stillness of the midnight,
Echoes from the past I hear;
Old time singing, gladness bringing,
From that lovely land somewhere.

As I travel on life's pathway,
Know not what the years may hold,
As I ponder, hope grows fonder,
Precious mem'ries flood my soul.

Memories at Grandpa's Farm

Joy is the presence of God in our lives which brings music to our souls.

For many years we prepared several days in advance for the summer-time journey of 1000 miles to Grandpa's farm in Indiana. There were most pleasant activities to do there and we knew we would not entertain one dull moment.

Cousins that lived in the community would come early each day we were there, which added to the memorable vacation. Grandma often prepared her grandchildren's favorite lunch of macaroni and cheese. She listened diligently to each child read or tell her stories and visited with these loved ones like they were adults. At times, dads would hoist a few children up into Grandpa's big semi-truck for a short ride to the gas station.

Everyone knew the most favored activity of all was about to happen when they saw Grandpa backing the garden tractor from the shed. This meant he would tie the little red wagon onto the back and one by one, the children would get their turn to ride.

One particularly hot, sunny day, it was finally time for 4-year-old Christa and her 2-year-old cousin, Lavern, to ride. We mom's plopped these young ones into the wagon and with a lurch, the make believe train started off. Excited giggles were heard all the way to the house as the little wagon train traveled around and around the yard. Grandpa was ready to quit well before the toddlers were, but when the trek did finish, the two little ones were quietly relaxed and ready for a well-needed nap.

These were only tiny happenings, but they are still important to remember. It's called making family memories. Listening to Grandma visit with her grandchildren like they were adults taught me loads about how I wanted to relate to my own grandchildren in years to come. ꙮ

Children's children are the crown of old men.
~ Proverbs 17:6 KJV ~

Congregation of Children

People — reaching out and reaching up — that is the church.

Just outside the back door of Grandma's large farmhouse lay the oversized sandbox where a shed had stood many years ago. The foundation remained and mounds of sand were piled inside the 24 by 30-foot cement form.

You can imagine the hours of fun this sand pile held for the some thirty plus grandchildren down through the years. Young boys built roads while fields were plowed in straight even rows and farms were established. Tractor motors roared loudly as a team of boys went off to work a few of the fields. Little girls sat in the corner created for the house, preparing mud pies for the busy working men.

This pack of children, often seven to ten in the sandbox at one time, fervently worked, shared and played together. Quiet conversations could be heard as they discussed and debated issues at hand. Now and then a squabble broke out; however, together the cousins managed to get it settled and the group remained best friends.

I caught a glimpse of the body of Christ as I considered these children at play. A small congregation, feverishly working and sharing together, edifying and encouraging one another for the cause of Christ. A team of two or three sent out for a certain project — ministering and blessing another. A differing opinion here and there followed by a coming together, forgiving and moving forward; conversing on messages from the Lord and His Word. These hours of make believe adult play in the sandbox will hopefully be the beginnings of learning virtues for the many important people-relating years ahead. 🌿

Let everyone of us please his neighbor for his good to build him up.
~ Romans 15:2 ~

Scrumptious Snack

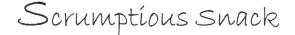

*The smallest deed is better than
the greatest intention!*

Coming for a visit my nephew Jon said, "I'll bring the snack for the evening, it's going to be walking tacos." That suited my fancy just grand, as one less item to prepare in the kitchen was always a welcome treat. Actually, I had never heard of walking tacos, but they sounded wonderful.

While Bob and I needed to be away for a few hours Jon, his wife Alice, son Jerry and Carla busied themselves in the kitchen preparing this quick, light and scrumptious snack. Upon our return home, everything was ready and setting on the counter. There were no plates set out, so I quickly went to the drawer to retrieve some when Jon said, "No Donna, plates are not needed." This said, I entrusted the snack to my guests, stood with my family as they gathered around the table and listened as Jon explained the details. Following is the recipe for a quick evening picnic, a camping expedition or a winter party.

Walking Tacos

1 cup guacamole	10 small bags Corn chips
1 cup sour cream	2 cups salsa
2 cups chopped lettuce	1/2 cup chopped onion
2 pound hamburger fried	2 cup shredded cheese
and prepared with taco seasoning mix	

Set each item on counter along with any additional taco toppings you might like. Crush chips in the bag while bags remain sealed. Open the bag along the top. Spoon toppings of your choice into the bag, mix together with a fork and enjoy.

*Because nothing is better for a man under the sun
then to eat, drink and be glad.*
~ Ecclesiastes 8:15 ~

A Day in the Big Woods

What we learn with pleasure we never forget –
~ Alfred Mercier ~

My nephew Joe and his four-year-old son Terry set out to help their friend, Chris, with his maple syrup endeavor. Chris' wife Mary had been in a tragic accident some weeks earlier that had left her paralyzed as a quadriplegic. Mary had been a major player in the syrup industry each year, but at this particular time, she lay in the hospital recovering from her severe injuries. Thus, the neighborhood collected together to give this kind couple a hand.

The chaps helping out were mainly elderly, retired farmers except for Joe and young Terry. One jolly crew of older men, along with the two younger members of the group, went around through the woods collecting the overflowing buckets of sap and dumping it into a big container on the horse-drawn wagon. Terry found it fascinating that these horses knew exactly how far to go, and exactly when to stop without anyone holding the reins. He diligently observed and studied each element of this part of the maple syrup industry, asking questions as they joggled along.

After a time, Terry wearied of riding the sap wagon and opted to stay with the other set of grandpas who were boiling the liquid down in the sugar shanty. The men mused over the knowledge the little man had of the syrup making process and the help he was to them. He chatted and discussed right along with the rest of the busy workers.

Early in the afternoon on that busy day, a home school mom and her children stopped by for an impromptu field trip. The team of men at the sugar shanty told her they were too busy keeping the sap boiling to show the family through the big woods. "But," they assured this kind mother, "Young Terry could handle the position of tour guide very well."

Proudly, Terry led the family way back into the woods, winding here and there, in and around large maple trees. He pointed out the sap buckets and explained the details of drilling the holes into the trees then placing spickets in the holes and hanging buckets properly on the hooks. "The sap knows to come from the tree to the spicket and drip into the pail that's waiting to be filled," he added. Terry also knew how to find the team of horses as he meandered through those big woods, expounding the whole way. Coming towards the sap wagon, you can imagine how surprised his dad was to observe his young son doing a splendid job of managing this field trip of eager students.

The grandpa's delighted in watching the young boy, declaring he's learning well above anything he'd have acquired in a structured school setting. Mrs. Home School Mom exclaimed over their good instructor and all the wonders they had gleaned from their excursion at Chris' maple syrup farm. ✒

Carry each other's burdens, and
in this way you will fulfill the law of Christ.
~ Galatians 6:2 ~

Mommy's Last Day of Work

The mother's heart is the child's schoolroom.
~ Henry Ward Beecher ~

While I was visiting my sister in Michigan, my mother and her youngest granddaughter, Megan, came to lunch. As we were eating, four-year-old Megan excitedly announced, "Today is mommy's last day at work!" Noting her enthusiasm, I said, "Oh, so what will she do then?" To that Megan exuberantly replied, "She's going to stay home with me!"

I wondered to myself if anyone brings greater joy to a toddler than her very own mother. Megan has loved going to grandma's house a couple of days each week, that's true; but none of that enjoyment matched the enthusiasm I heard in her voice when she declared, "She's going to stay home with me."

She watches over the affairs of her household.
~ Proverbs 31:27 ~

Pleasantries of Home

Bob and I had made a quick trip to Indiana for a visit with his family and spent the night with his sister Carol and her family of six children. I find coming to this home that is bouncing with activity, a reminder of my days gone by.

I slept a little late the next morning and wandered upstairs as everyone was sitting at the table for breakfast. Thirteen-year-old Aaron was fixing the french toast and asking if anyone would like an egg. The other five children, ages 2 to 12 sat around the table politely entering into conversation as they desired.

When the meal was finished, Josh, 10, cleared the table while Rebecca, 6, filled the sink with water. Four-year-old Adam stood on a stool at the rinsing sink and Joel, 12, took the tea towel in hand and began to dry the dishes. There was no fuss, no muss, no raised voices nor bickering. When Josh finished clearing the table, he pulled the chairs back away from it, got the broom and swept the kitchen floor.

Like the many other times we stop in here, I once again recalled back to when I was a young girl and lived in a house full of people. Nine children and my parents made us eleven plus there was often a foster child or two or a visitor. In a family this size, the after dinner routine was important to follow unless we prefered choas. We knew who was to wash dishes each night, who was to clear the table and who to dry. The floor needed swept three times a day and one was assigned to that task as well. Often my sisters and I would sing delightful songs like *Precious Memories* or *Supper time* as we whiled away the clean up hour.

Maybe those warm thoughts are a part of the reason I enjoy coming to this large family home. I always leave encorged and excited to tell my daughters, who are eagerly learning parenting how to's, all about this well-trained large household. How true, as the old hymn repeats, "There is beauty all around, when there's love at home."

Let us not be weary in well doing: for in due season
we shall reap, if we faint not.
~ Galatians 6:9 KJV ~

Suppertime
Ira Stamphill

Oh, many years ago in days of childhood.
I used to play till evening shadows come.
Then, winding down an old familiar pathway.
I heard my mother call at set of sun.

(Chorus)
Come home, come home, it's supper time.
The shadows lengthen fast.
Come home, come home it's supper time
We're going home at last.

One day beside her bedside I was kneeling.
And angel wings were winnowing the air.
She heard the call for suppertime in heaven,
And now I know she's waiting for me there.

In visions now I see her standing yonder,
And her familiar voice I hear once more.
The banquet table's ready up in heaven.
It is supper upon the golden throne.

Epilogue

Mother's Heart of Treasure

I wandered into my daughter's office today and noted something looked different. On her computer monitor neatly taped where she could see it every time she looked at the screen was a note.

Always interested in my daughters' hearts, I stepped over for a closer look. As I read down through the words my spirit burst with yet another treasure. A treasure to savor for eternity.

Carla is 28 years old. She's never been married. She's never bore her own children. The dreams that danced in her playtime and heart down through the years about a family of her own haven't come to pass. I've watched her struggle though coming to acceptance of her heavenly Father's plan.

While Rachel and Christa are busily homemaking and mothering, Carla is using her mothering ability to care for and nurture children in a different way. She taught school for many years and mentored students like they were her own. She's given care to dozens of children, including special needs little ones, and shared a mother's love with each one.

However, planted in the soul of most every woman is the longing to have a husband and children of her own. That same desire remains for Carla. Dearest to my heart though, is to know Carla is at rest. The reading I read taped on her computer monitor instilled a treasure in the depths of my being that will be there for a lifetime. Her best friend is the Lord Jesus and she trusts His ever-wise leading:

In His ever-gentle way Jesus wants to lift us up on His lap,
wrap His big strong arms around, wipe away our tears of longing
and pain, and whisper in our ears,
"It's all right, little child. Just rest your head on
My shoulder. I will take care of you. This world is
always in a hurry, but I teach My children patience.
Live, expecting a full and joyous life. And learn to trust
My perfect timing so that you may discover that all the pain found in
waiting has a magnificent and awesome purpose."

For each of my daughters to learn the message of Psalm 16:5, that whatever their lot to there with be content fulfills the prayers, yearnings, and burden of my heart down through the years.

About the Author

Donna Zook Kauffman was born into a Mennonite family and raised on a dairy farm in central Michigan. It was in the sprawling farm house that she recalls hearing the hymn *It May Not Be On the Mountain's Height* playing on the family's old record player. Each time the words rang, "It may not be on the mountain's height, Or over the stormy sea; My Lord will have need of me," quietly in her heart, she feared where the Lord might call her. The song continued to demand, "I'll go where you want me to go, dear Lord, Over mountain, or plain, or sea," and Donna would solemnly and determinedly say to the Lord, "Yes, Lord, I'll go where you want me to go, (but please not far away from my family)." She continued to sing along obediently though, "I'll say what you want me to say, dear Lord, I'll be what you want me to be."

She married Bob in 1973. Carla was 4 months old when the family followed the Lord's call and traveled 1000 miles to northern Ontario, Canada. To Donna, with a tiny baby in tow, this felt very far away. But God's call on her life and Bob's for sharing the message of the gospel for a lifetime was for real. They would go where He wanted them to go.

Two more little girls joined the family, Rachel was15 months behind Carla, and Christa three years after Rachel. They spent 17 rewarding years in Ontario. The Lord then led the family back closer to home, where at present, she and her husband, Bob, live in Parkman, Ohio. Bob pastors Agape Mennonite Assembly and manages a Corian countertop shop business.

Donna loves spending time with her three daughters and three grandchildren. She assists Bob in the ministry, and leads Bible Study groups continuing to follow the call of long ago. She is a freelance writer and has had articles published or accepted for publication in History's Women, Christian Mirror.com, Christian Families Online, Healthy Family, Companions, Purpose, Mennonite Brethren Herald, Georgia Home Education Association, Joyful Noise and a book entitled, *To Us By Us For Us.*

Ordering Information:

Donna Kauffman
19151 Hobart Road
West Farmington, Ohio 44491

1-440-548-5436

E-mail: kauffman@modex.com